Spiritual Master

Michael Beloved

Spiritual Master

Proof-reading Editors:
-     Marcia Beloved, tlb.

Cover Art + Final diagrams:
-     Michael Beloved

Graphics Editor + Lord Shiva Art:
-     Sir Paul Castagna

Financial Outlay
-     Śrīman Bharat Patel

Correspondence: **Email:**
Michael Beloved   axisnexus@gmail.com
3703 Foster Ave
Brooklyn NY 11203 USA
ISBN

978-0-9819332-3-8

LCCN

2009904389

Editorial appreciations:

This book was produced after 40 years of accepting, rejecting, accommodating and benefiting from spiritual masters. The author is in several lineages of gurus. Initially this book was reviewed by Śrīman Bhaktitīrtha Swāmī who is now deceased. He took a post as a spiritual master in a Vaishnava succession and was in discussion with the writer concerning this book. His admittance to the fallacies and sets-backs of gurus provided an impetus for revealing these ideas.

Table of Contents

Introduction

If you can make it through the spiritual journey without a spiritual master, then all good luck to you. Even Buddha, a pioneer of the spiritual quest took help from others initially. With their help he progressed, though not far enough, and not deep enough into spirituality, for his liking.

Spiritual life is hazardous because whenever one submits to another person, the nature of the association might border on exploitation in either direction, from spiritual master to disciple or from disciple to spiritual master.

This book is a warning to all those who act as spiritual masters, gurus, ministers, pastors, priests, counselors, therapists, psychiatrists, psychologists and the like. It is an invaluable aid to those who must acquire their help. With this information, you may approach such authorities, get the disciplines you require, and make progress without being hurt in the association.

*This book advises you how to become **a spiritual master without disciples**, a somebody without exploiting others, without the arrogance, the pomp and glory which is much desired by many who assume the position of Spiritual Master.*

Chapter 1

Types of Spiritual Masters

Absolute Person

The absolute spiritual master is someone who is a member of the Godhead, the set of individual entities who comprise cosmic creative powers and who remain aloof from material existence even when they appear in the material world. There are differing ideas about this in the literature which comes from India, but in the Bhagavad Gītā, Krishna revealed Himself as the Supreme Person among the absolute persons.

Does this mean that Godhead is plural? It does imply that. In fact when Krishna revealed the Supreme Person to Arjuna, there was a range of divine and semi-divine persons in the absolute range. Krishna clarified that He was the ultimate person. Elsewhere in the Bhagavad Gītā, Krishna explained that there were three categories of personalities: those whose status is affected by environments, those who remain unaffected regardless of environmental pressure, and the supreme one who is beyond the affected and unaffected entities. He rated Himself as the foremost of those who are unaffected.*

---

*These two types of spirits are in this world, namely the affected ones and the unaffected ones. All mundane creatures are affected. The stable soul is said to be unaffected.
But the highest spirit is in another category. He is called the Supreme Spirit, Who having entered the three worlds as the eternal Lord, supports it.
Since I am beyond the affected spirits and I am even higher than the unaffected ones, I am known in the world and in the Vedas as the Supreme Person. (Bhagavad Gītā 15.16-18)

In Christianity we are presented with the idea of a divine being who has a special son-to-father relationship with God. In Judaism we were introduced with the idea of God as supreme father. Judaism does not admit that God takes human form, rather they explain that God is spirit only and does not manifest materially. But in the history we are told that Moses saw the feet of God.

The question is: If God cannot manifest materially how did a human being see God through a human body? What is the possibility?

There are numerous puzzles in the various religions; some of these will be dealt with conclusively in this book. I will explain much on the basis of my familiarity with some religions as well as my religious and spiritual experience. Jesus Christ is great but we gain nothing by attaching imaginary accomplishments to him. Certainly for the past two thousand years, Christ effectively gave the world doses of cultural improvement, especially in terms of moral upliftment on the material plane, but that does not mean that he has liberated anyone from the material universe into the transcendence.

Can we imagine what sort of hell this world would be if the Europeans had set out to colonize the new world without first absorbing some of Jesus' influence? Even with His influence they committed atrocities, so we can just imagine the barbarity they would have enacted if there were no religious influence to rub their conscience.

If liberation means going to a heaven in the astral world where the material subtle bodies are hovering, then Christ has liberated many, at least temporarily, but if salvation means a complete migration from the gross and subtle material scene then Christ did very little indeed. And then, we may blame humanity and not Christ. Like other divine people, he tried, but our humanity fought long and hard and won out, to keep us earth bound.

In this book, I will discuss how spiritual parties are formulated, regulated, shrunk and expanded. Since spiritual masters are required and since nearly every scripture admits this, we cannot avoid spiritual authorities. But since to err is human, we must accept the humanity of these persons and protect ourselves from their mistakes.

I will now dismiss those philosophers who tell followers that a spiritual master is not required. If someone tells me that a spiritual master is not required and if I can accept that view, I am in effect accepting that person as my authority. Anyone who expresses such authority and is accepted by another, serves as a spiritual master.

The idea that a spiritual master has to be formally accepted or that he has to initiate a disciple before being regarded as an authority is a complete falsity but such a view prevails. Anytime I read a spiritual book or listen to a lecture on spiritual topics, I do, if I accept the ideas consciously or unconsciously, submit to the authority. The person acts in the capability of spiritual master regardless of whether I am formally related or not. In this book, I do not restrict the conversation to formal initiations and formal acceptances. Regardless of formality or the absence of it, the psychic influence of great personalities penetrates the human psyche.

Both in the East and West, it is believed that God, the Supreme Person or Supreme Being, is the ultimate spiritual master, the final authority, but the controversy concerns the name and activities of that God. Those who feel God is a person or those who regard Him as an ultimate force, are not necessarily in agreement as to exactly who God is or how He displays force. God is not clearly self-evident. Every human being has particular experiences which draw him (or her) into a particular belief pattern which changes as more experiences are integrated.

For instance, most Westerners who take to Eastern religions are persons who started this life with the belief in the Christian concept of God, a God that hardly any human being ever saw according to the Christian scripture, since that God is spiritually displayed only and does not manifest physically.

However even though they started at that point, they graduated to the Eastern view. Many of these Western graduates move from West to East only after having psychological experiences with mind-altering drugs. After taking such drugs and experiencing different dimensions, they could no longer settle for the fundamentalist Christian view. They went to the broader, experience-yielding mystic religions.

In India, the personalist believes that God is a perfect person with perfect non-erring qualities, the supreme Spiritual Master, the jagat-guru, the world authority. In some parts of India, Krishna is accepted; in others, Shiva, Durga, Buddha or other personalities who left their mark on the religious history of the East. Some regard these persons as facets of the one Supreme God.

In India those who do not believe that God is a person but who regard the Supreme as a force or as the sum total reality at large, usually accept a guru also but they accept one who advocates a godless doctrine. This belief is regarded as impersonal, nondual or atheistic depending on the particular idea. Still in that situation the problems of the guru-disciple relation exist just as it does in the personalistic religions. The problem is not the doctrine but the interaction of human nature.

In the view of the Vaishnavas, Krishna or alternately Vishnu is regarded as the Supreme Personality. According to the legends which describe Krishna, He was accepted by some as a deva or demigod, as only one of the gods. He was accepted by others as a powerful politician, as an expansion of the God, Vishnu. Some regard Him as the Supreme Person in a Plural Godhead. It depends on the traditional beliefs and experiences of the person involved.

Krishna's father, Vasudev, accepted Krishna as an incarnation of the God, Vishnu. Krishna's foster father, Nanda, also regarded Krishna as such on the basis of what he was told by the authoritative priest Garga, and also by the miracles performed by the infant and juvenile Krishna. Others in

Krishna's time rejected Krishna's claim. Duryodhan, a powerful prince who was a rival of Krishna's friends, the Pandavas, heard about Krishna from authorities like His great-uncle, the statesman Bhishma, and from the religious authority Vyasa but Duryodhana regarded Krishna as a powerful mystic only. Persons like Shishu and Danta accepted Krishna as a dark-skinned cowherd, guerilla warrior, who somehow or other got political power.

Therefore, even in Krishna's time, His asserted divinity was in question, what to speak of reaching back to the old scriptures to prove His claims made in the Bhagavad Gītā. Evidence can be collected from anywhere but direct evidence is a different matter. Human history is not that uniform where we can prove things in a universal way by citing an ancient text. Records of human history before the modern era are haphazard. Educated people generally consider such history to be unreliable legends. If anything, Krishna's divinity may be accepted on the basis His Bhagavad Gītā discourse, just as the life of Christ may be accepted at face value according to his explanations in the New Testament.

Regardless of whether we can stomach these ancient texts from India, the Near East and elsewhere, the human need for spiritual masters remains. The question of finding a Supreme Person is on-going. Until we can prove conclusively that there is no such person or that there is such **singularity** as an absolute origin, the questions will remain.

According to the *Mahabharata* story, just before the battle of Kurukshetra there was some doubt about Krishna's position as the Supreme Person. To establish Himself for all time, Krishna spoke the Gītā, where in theory and practice, He revealed supremacy over the ordinary and extraordinary personalities.

The problem with the evidence is this: Only the theory is presented in the discourse with Arjuna, because merely hearing about the experiences of the Universal Form of Krishna which Arjuna saw, does not in any way cause a person to objectively see that Form. Some say that they are convinced merely by hearing about Arjuna's experience, but Arjuna himself was not convinced even after hearing nine chapters of discourse (chapters 2 through 10) from Krishna, after which he cleared up his issue with Krishna by stating:

> The origin and ruination of the beings was heard of in detail by me, O Person Whose eyes are shaped like lotus petals. You also described Your eternal majestic glory.
>
> This is as You explained about Yourself, O Supreme Lord. I wish to see Your Majestic Form, O Supreme Person.
>
> If You think that it is possible for me to see this, O Lord, Master of the yoga technique, then make me see You in that Eternal Form. (Bhagavad Gītā 11.2-4)

Thus those who feel that Krishna should be accepted as the Supreme God without visual evidence, may explain why Arjuna was not convinced until he saw Krishna's control on the supernatural and spiritual planes of existence.

Spiritual masters are part and parcel of human society. We must deal with them, take help from them and risk being cheated by them as well. In turn, they must face us, instruct us, and be imperiled by us. This transpires. This book is presented to reduce the amount of exploitation by spiritual masters and the amount of victimization they suffer in return by accepting disciples.

In this book, Krishna will be used as the example of an absolute spiritual master. We could have selected the Christian deity since that deity is accepted in Judaism and Islam alike. We are not fanatical about Krishna. On the contrary until a person gets spiritual experience of a divinity, all their ideas about that person are mental constructions only.

Dealing with the Absolute Person as the spiritual master is advantageous, particularly in the sense that one might not have to approach another authority. While, in dealing with lesser authorities, one invariably has to take help from others. But believing that one's deity is the Supreme Person for the purpose of offsetting one's insecurities is an entirely different way of approaching the subject of submitting to an authority. If that absolute person does not manifest on the human level, one is left to the device of mystic or spiritual communication and that involves the inaccuracies of the human mind.

Semi-absolute spiritual masters

While in the Eastern countries there is some idea of many divine beings, in the Western setting the idea of multiple gods is ridiculed and shunned. In Judaism there is God and the prophets, in Christianity there is God and the son of God, and in Islam there is God and the last prophet.

Christianity presents the Absolute God and the semi-absolute son of God. For all practical purposes, this son of God is presented as God. In some Eastern religions, there is a range of semi-absolute persons. Some contend, for instance, that Krishna is the Vishnu God and is therefore semi-absolute in reference to Shiva. But those who extol Vishnu or Krishna as the Primal Person, list Shiva as the semi-absolute person. It is not a point of contention in this book. It does not matter to me if Jesus Christ or Krishna or Shiva or anyone else is the Supreme God.

Before, I posited Krishna as the Absolute Person. Now I will posit Shiva as the semi-absolute Person. This is only to make the case of the relationship between spiritual masters and disciples. We could have placed Jesus Christ, for instance, as God. We do not care which one of these persons are proven to be God. That is not the issue. Whosoever is proven to be God will have to be admitted when that proof is forthcoming. It makes no difference if the Christian deity, or alternately a Hindu deity proves to be supreme. The submission to that Supreme Person will be the issue then, not the identity of the Person.

The semi-absolute being is not a limited person who is constrained by material existence. As such, for all practical purposes, he or she is very close in quality to Godhead, at least in terms of detachment from material influence and precise mystic perception. Another special attribute of theirs which singles them out from the limited beings is their ability to create their own spiritual territories. Usually these semi-absolute people do not lose the spiritual focus. They are to a greater extent immune from the effects of vices.

We get some understanding of this immunity by a statement made by Krishna, where He told Arjuna in the Gītā that He appeared visibly in the material setting and so also did Arjuna, but Krishna said that He remembered their previous appearances while Arjuna forgot all about them. Krishna said that He is birthless and imperishable and is factually the Lord of all beings, but He appears in the material world through His own supernatural power by controlling various forms of nature through which he becomes perceptible to human beings.

The semi-absolute beings are also immune to lower influences but not to the degree of the absolute ones. Still, those semi-absolute people are much more immune than the limited beings who struggle to establish a resistance to lower existence. Usually a limited being does not remember former births but that does not mean there is no memory within the psyche. The memory is in the psyche but it can only be perceived if one is shifted to a higher plane.

If one's spiritual master is a semi-absolute person, one would be inspired and energized but still one has to take up disciplines, otherwise the boost in power awarded would not be maintained in one's nature.

A conditioned soul does not necessarily thrive if moved to a better existential environment; he may actually suffer in such a higher situation if he is not properly prepared. If one takes a lowly, dirty man into a very clean place and asks him to function there in hygienic cleanliness, the man might suffer from the austerity required and he might fail to maintain himself. Thus he will long to return to the lower environment. One should be groomed for higher association. Some spiritual masters, in all eagerness and sincerity, convey the idea that once one gets a higher taste one will stick to it. This kind of statement is mostly hype, because human experience speaks to the contrary.

In practical life, we find that when a person is given a higher experience he or she invariably returns to the lower relations. The higher experience does not entirely remove the lower nature. One has to endeavor to remove the lower attachments. The idea that one can instantly reach and then remain at the higher level is a false one only. One may instantly get to a higher level and get a higher taste but one cannot endure there; one must either return to the lower place and stagnate there or one must return there and endeavor by some means to return to the higher plane.

In 1972 I lived in a yoga ashram where I learnt some methods of breath infusement in kundalini yoga. At that time the teacher of discipline lived far away. His advanced student held the classes. After some time, this advanced student abandoned his wife and went to live in an apartment with a much younger woman. After this the spiritual master of the society came to the ashram. When questioned about the action of the advanced disciple he was at loss for a reply. Then he said, "I myself do not understand it. He was married by religious rites. Now he left his wife and is living with another. What can I do?"

This is one case of getting a higher experience of marriage by religious formality and then returning to the permissive habit of having sex casually without maintaining former commitments. In other words, the righteous way of resisting adultery was pushed aside for lower habit.

In yet another case, this writer in the year 1982, lived at a Vaishnava temple in the United States. The leader of the temple was an advanced disciple of an Indian Vaishnava spiritual master. During the conversation with his associates, the leader boasted that some followers of a Vedanta group could not follow the regulative principles and that they smoked cigarettes. He said, "We follow the principles. We are reformed of past habits. As soon as we met our spiritual master, we gave up all bad habits."

Later on, however, this same advanced disciple was imprisoned for racketeering and was implicated in the murders of other disciples of his spiritual master. In addition, he was rejected by his followers on account of pedophile activities. He criticized others from a rival group but he did not realize at the time that the higher taste did not completely remove his lower habits which were simply dormant for the time being and were reasserted later, causing him to be rejected by his parent society.

The divine association may be given; in fact it is being given, but we either reject it or take it cheaply. Therefore it does not stay with us continuously. As a result we are sometimes in and sometimes out of the lower habits, alternately.

A semi-absolute person can give a boost of energy to a disciple or can cause a revelation of higher realities, but for permanence in this, the disciple must complete the supportive austerities. A disciple who is unable to do this will inevitably return to lower planes and will again be shifted back into lower realities.

Limited spiritual masters

Among the limited beings there are various levels of spiritual autonomy, such that one person may be a ward for thousands of souls and another may only be responsible for a few. This implies that some limited entities are no match to others who are also in the limited category. Some rate Jesus Christ as a limited spiritual master, even though in the New Testament, he is accredited as being co-existent with the Absolute God

The limited spiritual masters are those who are directly empowered, by an absolute or semi-absolute being. The empowerment may be temporary or perpetual. Limited personalities are usually empowered with a specific potency only. In the *Mahabharata* legends, Arjuna is an example of a person empowered for a limited time only. He was empowered not as a spiritual master but as a warrior in the support and upkeep of righteous behavior. He was never famous as a spiritual master. Thus the empowerment usually applies in particular areas only. The entity is empowered for a particular purpose and in some cases, the empowerment may be removed quickly, sometimes gradually, and sometimes it remains a permanent feature. It is indicated in the Bhagavad Gītā that Arjuna's empowerment as a law and order enforcer is a repeated empowerment because Lord Krishna cited His own and Arjuna's previous appearances. But there are cases where one is empowered for the time being with a particular power which may never be boosted into one's nature again.

Since the empowered souls have a particular potency or ability, they specialize in a particular area and therefore anyone who takes their association may get special techniques from them. These empowered souls may give practical assistance to their disciples but the disciples also have to take up needed disciplines and become purified by self effort, in order to permanently upgrade the lower nature.

Some of the empowered entities are eternally-liberated. Some are souls who strove for liberation and attained the goal or who are still striving and are partially-perfected only. In so far as they are perfected in particular phases of spiritual discipline, they give practical techniques which worked for them. The rest of their association has to do with dispersion of the ideas which may or may not give the intended results.

If one is serious in spiritual life, one should find an empowered entity who mastered the particular technique required for salvation; otherwise one will get general methods which do not yield full purification and which cause one to stagnate.

Empowered disciples of limited authorities

The spiritual master who is merely a disciple of empowered souls cannot liberate anyone. That person can bring one as close to liberation as he or she experienced; that person can put one in touch with his or her senior authority who is higher. It is a fact, however, that someone who is empowered may pretend not to be and may pose as a disciple of an authority.

A limited being can only deliver spiritual experiences in so far as he or she experienced, while the rest of discourse is lip service to things which he or she heard or knowledge acquired in religious books. The actual experience is potent and the rest is mostly talk even if it is repeated confidently.

A description of something does not guarantee the experience of reality, even though some spiritual masters claim otherwise. Specific techniques are required. Spiritual life cannot be merely a matter of hearing, and then forming ideas based on what is heard. Hearing is the beginning of spiritual life. Direct experience is the median level. Total transference is the final phase. In many instances, the idea one forms after hearing is at variance with the reality being described. Experience is required to validate hearing. Those who merely repeat what the spiritual master said, without having realized through experience, fail to determine whether his words were based on truth or were distorted. They cannot deliver his message with potency except with a type of mock conviction.

When a spiritual master tells a disciple something that is true on a higher level and does not or is unable to convey the actual experience to the disciple, and then instructs the disciple to repeat exactly as he said, the spiritual master is in effect saying that he can only describe the experience but not relate or convey direct perception of it. In other words, he diplomatically admits that he does not have the power to convey the experience. Therefore the disciple has to settle for a description only and this creates a problem in that the description becomes distorted as soon as it makes contact with the mind of the disciple. This happens due to the nature of the mind.

If a man visits New York City and then goes to South America to visit aborigines, he may describe his New York experience. He may instruct the natives to repeat the description verbatim. However this does not mean that the natives experienced it. Unless the traveler can take the natives to New York directly, the conveyance of information remains incomplete. Furthermore the natives will formulate misconceptions which they will convey to others. They cannot stop the distortion because that is the nature of the mind. Therefore there is nothing like direct experience even though spiritual masters from every type of group and every belief, carefully cover up and usher away their inadequacy, by insisting that followers be satisfied by hearing of transcendence only.

In some societies, these spiritual masters are so effective in their way of delivery without conveying the actual experience, that the followers become hostile to experience and reject anyone who might show an interest beyond mere hearing. Traditionally in India, everything begins by accepting a spiritual master. One hears from the teacher, one serves as stipulated, and one learns by associating. Although hearing is the basic way to begin spiritual life, it is not the total method.

Self declared spiritual masters

Perhaps the most important aspect in locating a spiritual master is our need for a reliable guide. Is the spiritual master such a person? Supposing he or she is, then there arises a more important consideration; that of the validity of his or her promises. All systems of belief are symptomatic of promises which cannot all be fulfilled immediately. Thus even if an authority is reliable, how real is the doctrine? Thus there are two factors to observe:

- ## The reliability of the spiritual master

- ## The practicality of his doctrine

If only one of these is valid, then the whole system is useless. For there to be success, both must be substantiated in the life of the follower.

Among the various types of spiritual masters, there are the self-declared ones who chalk out a new path of salvation and offer it to humanity. These self-declared personalities either create their own system afresh or they blend already existing processes into a new mixture. For instance, Buddha created his own system, propagated it effectively and established solid opposition to the tradition of his time. Guru Nanak created a system of religion in the Adi Grantha text which is a mixture of compatible Muslim and Hindu aspects. Nanak took compatible ideas and experiences of both systems and created Sikhism. And there are others who take parts of an existing system or religion, distort these and create a new religion afresh without any loyalty or credit to the original methods.

If we study most of the prominent religions, we will find that in each case, the authority took something from an existing system, adjusted, built up and changed it to a greater or lesser degree. There is no exception to this.

In the writer's view, the most definite and authoritative book of religion is the Bhagavad Gītā. Even in that text, we find that Krishna took selected parts of the traditional system of His time and then rejected other portions. For instance, Lord Krishna rejected parts of the Veda that glamorize the aspects of material nature and cultural activities. He accepted the Upanishadic authorities who spoke of the temporary and permanent types of reality.

In the case of Jesus Christ, he took much from the Mosaic tradition and from the teachings of Abraham and their prophets but he rejected the traditional, Jewish, racial approach. He rejected the established priestly tradition and caused his disciples to supersede the existing priestly hierarchy.

In the Vaishnava system in India, Chaitanya accepted the ideas of the Madhva lineage in a general sense and carefully separated Himself from some of their views, but at the same time he identified with that lineage as being part of the lineage which he accepted.

The examples are there. In a sense, every spiritual master of repute is a self-declared authority. Let us take Krishna. In His own time, some accepted Him at best as an incarnation of God, others took Him to be empowered and others took Him to be a powerful historic personality of human origin. At Kurukshetra, Krishna emphatically and suddenly dispelled all these views when He showed Arjuna and others His Universal Form and caused Arjuna to claim Him as the God of gods. In a frightful mood, seeing awful visions regarding Lord Krishna's universal control and seeing Krishna's power struggle with opponents everywhere on the supernatural plane, Arjuna adopted a respectful mood and glorified Krishna as the master of the cosmic manifestation.

Jesus established himself through miracles by healing the sick, causing recently-departed souls to reenter and animate their dead bodies, miraculously reproducing foodstuffs and feeding crowds. In the end he submitted to a crucifixion. When asked by the judge if he was the king of Jews, Jesus said that he was, even though, in fact, he was not the king in the physical or social sense. Thus his efforts to declare himself as a spiritual authority were rejected in his own time.

Assuming that reincarnation is a fact, assuming that the spirits are eternal, usually one cannot recognize a person's identity from the past life or lives. A spiritual master must establish himself afresh in each life. A certain amount of self declaration is always required, but some do it subtly and others, blatantly.

Chapter 2

Functions of

Spiritual Masters

Functions of the absolute figures

In the some Sanskrit literature, the absolute figure is addressed as the Person God, Vishnu, meaning the One who maintains the cosmos. In some other texts, the Absolute is presented as the Person God Shiva, with His cosmic destructive powers. And in yet other tests, the Person God has cosmic creative capacity as Brahma.

These are rated as divinities. If we accept this information at face value, it would mean that the Person God must be capable of creating, maintaining and demolishing these creations. Incidentally in the Vedic system, a goddess named Devi is attributed as the Person God. She is said to have the creative, sustaining and demolishing power over the creation.

So what would such a Person God do if He or She were to take a material body? For what reason would the Person God take such a demeaning body? Would His or Her divinity be compromised in the descent? The first consideration is the effect of such an appearance on the divinity concerned. In the sectarian legends of Krishna, Shiva, Brahma and Devi, there is a distinct and careful presentation that these persons are not undone by assumption of a physical form. The most popular legend is perhaps, the one about Krishna. He explained how He was not affected when using a physical body:

Even though I am birthless and My person is imperishable, and even though I am the Lord of the creatures, by controlling My material energies, I become visible by My supernatural power. (Bhagavad Gītā 4.6)

Krishna cited birthlessness and imperishability of His person, but prior to making this statement, He said that all individual spirits have those qualities, even though some do not recall their past:

This embodied soul is not born, nor does it die at any time, nor having existed will it not be. Being birthless, eternal, perpetual and primeval, it is not slain in the act of killing the body. (Bhagavad Gītā 2.20)

The Blessed Lord said: Many of My births transpired, and yours, Arjuna. I recall them all. You do not remember, 0 scorcher of the enemies. (Bhagavad Gītā 4.5)

The birthlessness and perpetuity has little significance to this inquiry of the effects endured by a divinity when taking a material body. For that we must consider Krishna's statement about controlling the material energies. If the God Person remains in divine status during a human decent, then He must have the power to control the energies which are involved in the creation of the gross form He would use during the advent.

The other consideration concerns the reason for the descent. Krishna explained His motives in this way:

For protecting the saintly people, to destroy the wicked ones, and to establish righteousness, I come into the visible existence from era to era. (Bhagavad Gītā 4.8)

In the interest of law and justice? For the protection of the law-abiding people?

One thing is certain, the way one perceives material existence when one is in the divine or celestial worlds, is completely different to the way one would see it if one were synchronized into material existence while using a material body. In my experience, there is no perception of material existence in a divine body. For some mundane perception, one has to use a subtle form comprised of subtle material energy, radio and light waves. I propose that a God Person must first descend to the subtle material level before He or She could even perceive what transpires in the material world. Even for expressing an interest in this world, the energy of interest must penetrate through subtle material energy before it can register in the gross world.

Persons who use divine bodies, spiritual forms, are not the only ones to exist after the mundane universes disappear but they are the only ones who objectively understand what transpires. They have the superior perspective, just as parents have maturity over infants in the crib. The infants hardly understand the activity in the world around them. They are dependent on the services of adults. Similarly all limited personalities in the material creation are overseen by those divinities.

Formerly in the Vedic setting, there was an understanding that the Vishnu, the Divinity, was one only. In other words, some great sages felt that there was only one God Person as the Divinity and that He came repeatedly to assist saintly people with social difficulties or to enlighten them. For instance, at the name-giving ceremony of Krishna, the informed priest, Garga, told Krishna's foster father that astrology and intuition indicated that Krishna appeared previously, once with a white complexion, then a red one, then yellow, and finally black, as the name Krishna indicated.

As far as Garga was concerned, the child Krishna was the same God appearing again but looking a bit different. These great sages like Garga were, however, incorrect in their perception because the Personality of Godhead is multiple and coordinated to one another, except for Krishna Who claims himself as the Supreme Person. We state this on the basis of Krishna's revelation of Himself, since we cannot prove it otherwise. This is stated on the basis of what Krishna said and on statements of reliable, great mystics like Arjuna, Narad, and Vyasa.

Recent teachers gave testimony but the testimony of Arjuna is prominent because Arjuna saw the Universal Form. He did not perceive the form by hearing. He saw it and drew conclusions on that basis. Narad and Vyasa also, had divine perceptions. For instance, Narad Muni toured Lord Krishna's palaces and personally saw the various parallel divine forms of Krishna functioning separately in different roles as variant heads of households.

The God Persons come for particular tasks in reference to their self-imposed obligations. As for accepting disciples, generally the God Persons do not accept many disciples. They come in a political family. For instance, the Ramayana legend tells us of Rama, the son of Dasharatha. Rama acted as a prince and king mostly and not as a spiritual master. He appeared in a ruling family. He remained in that role, even to the point of accepting others as spiritual advisors throughout His earthly appearance.

Krishna served as Arjuna's spiritual master on the battlefield but prior to that Krishna served as a prince and king in a ruling dynasty. In the juvenile years He served as a cowherd boy and not as the son of a guru. Krishna also introduced the idea of an absolute presence in the individual psyche, alongside the limited spirit who uses that psyche. This is how He described that indwelling absolute personality:

> *I will explain that which is to be experienced, knowing which one gets in touch with eternal life. The beginningless Supreme Reality is said to be neither substantial nor insubstantial.*
>
> *Everywhere is Its hands and feet, everywhere Its eyes, head and face, everywhere is Its hearing ability in this world; It stands, ranging over all.*

It has the appearance of having all sensual moods, and It is freed from sensuousness. Though unattached, It maintains everything. Though free from the influence of material nature, It is the experiencer of that influence nevertheless.

It is outside and inside the moving and non-moving beings. Because of Its subtlety, this beginningless Supreme Reality is not comprehended. This Reality is situated far away and is in the location as well.

It is undivided among the beings, but It appears as if It is divided in each. It is the sustainer of the beings and this should be known. It is the absorber and producer.

This is declared as the light of the luminaries, but It is beyond gross or subtle darkness. It is the information, the education and the goal of education. It is situated in the psychological core of all beings. (Bhagavad Gītā 13.13-18)

Krishna is Arjuna's eternal spiritual master but for others the Lord is the spiritual master directly only from His position as the Supersoul deep within the psyche, meaning that He cannot be reached by most people since most of us live and dwell on the periphery of the self, attending to bodily and social affairs. The average human being has no alternative but to seek an empowered soul as the spiritual master. By nature we are outward-going. We cannot reach deep into our nature. Therefore we take help from the empowered souls, who are more in touch with the divine.

Functions of the semi-absolute person with a cultural interest

Generally the semi-absolute person does not directly become the spiritual master of any earthly place. Like the divinities, they also work through agents. For instance in the Vedic legends, we are repeatedly told that a creative god named Brahma sends his mentally-conceived son, Narad, to do the teaching work. Brahma is involved in management duties on his celestial planet, in receiving respect and honor there, and in worshipping his deity. Therefore it is highly unusual for him to become a human being's spiritual master.

A celestial person functions from a celestial level. His main interest in human beings is cultural development, involving economic security, prosperity and good government. The semi-absolute persons remain as permanent residents of the celestial world. Their presence there imperceptibly attracts persons in this world. The attraction to any of them, is felt by human beings as a need to go to heaven or paradise after death. To satisfy a semi-absolute person and to gain his approval for celestial transport after death one has to live a pious life on earth or be affiliated and compliant with a religion which is propagated by one of his agents who serves as a religious figurehead on earth.

In a legend involving Brahma, a certain Kashipu performed austerities. He was able to make Brahma appear to him but only after he performed some very serious and exceptional disciplines for many years without interruption. In the case of Priyavarta, Brahma spoke to him briefly about assigned duties but only after Narad Muni instructed and helped Priyavarta. In most circumstances Brahma remains out of range of human endeavor and human mental power. He is remote.

Until one is purged of passionate and depressive powers, one cannot see Brahma nor can one rise to Brahma's planet.

Going to the kingdom of God is not a matter of wishful thinking. It is a matter of applying a definite technique that effectively purifies and completely removes lower traits in the psyche. It is not based on a religious precedent, belief or system that helps part of the time and fails part of the time. It is not based on promises of great preachers, ministers, pastors, priests, spiritual masters, gurus or sages, nor on wishful thinking and hopes for liberation. It is something more than that, requiring one to become purified before leaving the material body.

Before one can deal with Brahma or have a person in his category as one's spiritual master, one has to become a complete celibate. We see this in the case of Kashipu. He was ill-motivated but still at the particular time he attained full celibacy and totally restrained the sensual nature. Then Brahma came to him. In another case, the person Priyavarta was schooled in celibacy and then Brahma advised him to become a conditional celibate householder. In yet another case, there is the example of a person who fell away from Brahma's association. That was King Mahabhish, a king on this earthly planet. He became so elevated that he went to Brahma's planets and attended meetings there with various celestial officials, but it was his misfortune to see nudity of the goddess Ganga when her skirt blew up. He could not maintain the celibate stance during the goddess' exposure. As a result he came down to the earth and took a body as King Shantanu.

Getting a person like Brahma as a spiritual master directly, is for the most part a completely hopeless task, because we are not purified enough to attain such high association. We are too attached to lower planes. We do not have the stamina required to conquer the lower nature.

Another aspect of Brahma's relationship with disciples is that he is not particularly interested in liberating any of them. This same feature is present in many earthly spiritual masters, including some who pretend that they want to liberate their followers. Most of these spiritual masters are simply trying to form a corps of associates. They have absolutely no intention of helping anyone to full liberation. Brahma is looking for assistance with his duties as a universal cultural manager.

Work of the semi-absolute people with a spiritual interest

These authorities are primarily concerned to motivate a spiritual quest in anyone who uses a material body. Their idea is that the material bodies should be used to access spiritual existence and not just for the sake of cultural improvement on the material plane. They admit that a material body is necessary but they do not feel that one's life should be focused only on prosperity and enjoyment.

They encourage materialistic living only in so far as it would bring on a realization about the long term harm such living would cause for the person involved. Thus there is a conflict between these authorities and those who profess that one should try to gain as much as is imaginatively possible from material nature.

The semi-absolute beings with spiritual interest, keenly observe how we are frustrated in the many experiences we encounter in material existence. They wait for an opportunity to approach us to discuss the possibility of slackening our focus on mundane achievements. When we reach a stage of disgust, we become submissive to these beings, otherwise we avoid their reforming energy and continue in the quest for dominance in the material world.

Functions of empowered entities

These beings are neither ordinary nor extra-ordinary, being somewhere in-between. Their main interest is control of human societies. These act as politicians and as spiritual leaders. A few of them become wealthy merchants with vast political reach. From the onset, as soon they develop a material body they begin to exercise control, first over their parents, particularly over their mothers, and then over friends until at last in adult forms they assume a leadership position and take control over a sector of humanity.

The main work of the empowered spiritual master is to release the souls who are attracted to them and give a spiritual boost to a spiritually-deprived humanity. While the Absolute Figure works on a broader scale and serves to rectify wholesale injustices, the empowered spiritual masters are supposed to stick to the spiritual interest of mankind and to deal with social problems as a side feature. It is seen, however, that many of these teachers get caught up in the social affairs. Their missions become foreshadowed, lost as it were, in efforts at cultural improvement.

The problem has a two-fold basis. The first is the weakness of the empowered spiritual master. The second is poor human condition. Due to weakness and faulty communication with superiors who sent him to the human level, the empowered spiritual master becomes bogged down with human engagement, affections and sentiments. In the process they become greatly weakened. What began as a spiritual mission devolves into a social club between the master and disciples.

The vacant spiritual condition of humans is something the spiritual masters must contend with, since if the human beings have meager spiritual realization and resist sensual discipline, the teacher cannot deliver his message as intended. By necessity it is adapted and diluted considerably. By rendering such compassion, these gurus attune themselves more and more to human nature and begin to forget their superiors.

It is said that Bodhidharma left India and journeyed into China but when he got there he found that the people were too weak in spirit to take up the Buddhist doctrine which he came to preach. He developed a martial art technique and taught that instead. His idea was to strengthen them mentally by physical means. In the process many took to martial arts and did not take the Buddhist religion seriously. That was a situation of an adaptation to a poor human condition.

In the Vedic stories we learn that the empowered spiritual masters of worth came down from higher planets like Brahmaloka. When they get here, they have to deal with the degraded human condition. They must do some adjusting. Invariably, the empowered spiritual masters and their agents must adjust to accommodate the human condition.

If the empowered spiritual master finds that he cannot deliver his mission because the people cannot take his message in its original form, he must either scale down the original plan given to him by his superior or just work with a few selected human beings who might qualify. Scaling down the original plan means reducing the austerity involved and giving something that is practical and which will upgrade the followers sufficiently until they come to a higher level.

Essentially this problem of adjustment is the main headache for the spiritual masters. It causes departures from the original plan and makes the spiritual masters themselves deviate from their original purpose.

The empowered spiritual masters or their agents on earth, are usually empowered with a specific potency. Their followers are usually fond of one aspect of the spiritual upgrade only. For instance in spiritual life there is self-purification, reception of grace or divine qualities, preaching to the public, worshipping the chosen divine personality, serving the teacher, and making consistent overall progress in all these aspects simultaneously. However a particular spiritual master may stress just one aspect to the neglect of the others. He might be adept at an aspect, or a part of one aspect. His followers will master that phase only, and only to the degree of their absorption in the process.

Some spiritual masters stress self-purification above everything else. Their followers work on self-purification and have little practice of the other aspects, while other spiritual masters stress another part and neglect some other phase.

It is assumed that an empowered personality is resistant and will not stay down on a lowly level of material existence. Still, such a soul may fall and falter in a particular incarnation from which he must retrieve himself in the present or future life. By stating that he is eternally liberated we mean that he cannot remain satisfied with the lowly conditions of earthly existence because he feels that this is not his natural state. He will strive to retrieve himself even if he committed criminal acts and vices.

Those who are not resistant but who are serious about upgrading their existence run the risk of reaching certain high levels of advancement and then becoming satisfied with that progress. They open a preaching mission as spiritual teachers and pretend that they attained full perfection. Gradually they sink down in material existence. But even these aspiring souls who make the mistake of declaring themselves as fit spiritual masters, do again rise up after faltering in spiritual life. Their elevation is more gradual. It requires much more inspirational inducements from superiors. The eternally-liberated souls on the other hand, seem to get out mostly by their own endeavor since they instinctively know what to do to clean themselves of the criminality and vices which tinged them in a particular life.

An example of a resistant soul is Arjuna, His life shows how someone in his category may get bogged down periodically. Arjuna had two vices but Lord Krishna assured him of the godly nature. Arjuna's vices were those of sentimental affection and family attachment in social concerns. He was freed from these at Kurukshetra.

Another great devotee, an eternally-liberated soul who was caught in the same family attachment, was General Bhishma. He was delivered through his attraction to Lord Krishna, combined with his moral conscience and expertise in technical yoga practice. Arjuna became liberated by hearing the Bhagavad Gītā and by seeing the visual display of Lord Krishna's power. He was proficient in yoga practice and was expert at dimensional astral projection.

A case of a practicing devotee who reached a certain level and fell down because of vice is Ajamil. He was on a high level of purity but he cohabited with a prostitute. After she introduced him to sexual vices, he gave up good training and became degraded. Later he was rescued by divine people.

Once a seeker attains the position as a recognized spiritual leader, he is in a sense, doomed to failure because the overall influence coming from disciples and followers is itself degrading and accommodating of any pride the authority might have. Such pride leads to ruination.

A resistant soul has challenges ahead of him and a less-resistant soul has even more problems to face. The eternally-liberated souls come with a flash empowerment. They may carry with them their own developed power which is converted into mystic influence on the human plane. The flash empowerment comes from some great soul or from the divinity directly. It is meant for a particular purpose, to last only for a particular time. For instance, Arjuna had a flash empowerment to challenge opposing warriors on a broad basis at Kurukshetra. His mission was to confront warriors who opposed the ideas of Krishna. As such those who faced Arjuna at Kurukshetra and elsewhere were in fact facing the Almighty God directly. They had no chance of defeating him. He was like a needle point being driven by a colossal power. Later on however, the empowerment left him and he felt like an ordinary man, except for his affectionate relationship with Lord Krishna. He had yoga expertise and memory of the Bhagavad Gītā to lean on, to help him cross the chasm of bewildering circumstances.

Some of these resistant souls or their disciples get energy from the supernatural people who reside in the celestial world. By this, their charismatic power increases for a while and then it vanishes. When it increases, they appear to be irresistible, when it vanishes, they appear rejected, discolored and depressed.

Some are aware of the cause of the empowerment. Some are not. Power is transferred into the subtle body which is sprinkled by celestial nectar (amrita). It is a fact, however, that their fame in the world vanishes as soon as the effect is worn off.

There are many instances in the Vedic legends. For instance, Kashipu's body had completely deteriorated except for the bones. When a few drops of nectar fell on his surviving subtle form, a new attractive and irresistible material body was instantly created. A legend has it that Ravan also had nectar flowing all over his body except at his navel.

It does not matter if one is aware of it or not, if one's subtle body is rubbed with nectar, one will become charismatic and will, all of a sudden, get a large following, but it will only last for a while and then one will feel disempowered.

Under certain circumstances the empowerment seems so natural to the great souls that they forget the source of it and begin feeling that it is their power. Thus they make mistakes, costly mistakes, which cause a disproportionate sense of pride, leading to a downfall. At such times, the empowered entities may realize the mistake and practice austerities to rectify themselves.

The aspiring entities who become spiritual leaders also get some minor power but unfortunately such minor power may seem to be major in the eyes of followers. Then the leader becomes boastful and proud. He takes unnecessary risks, and then becomes overloaded with reactions which terminate in disgrace. He gradually becomes dried up and the disheartened followers abandon him. In this way he comes to his senses and begins to realize his limited sway.

In every art or science, there are certain tricks of the trade through which one attains success, develops a monopoly of a process and then uses that process to glorify oneself. In spiritual life there are also methods of aggrandizement.

One main trick is the technique of bringing power from a special past life. This means that in a past life, an authority performed austerities to develop charismatic power. He acquires a new body with the reserved power but he pretends that he is naturally divine. He flashes himself on human society. This trick has to do with hiding the austerities from the past life. If a spiritual master develops himself in austerity in the eyes of the people, then it will be known that he became powerful by a particular practice. Perceptive people will then seek him, not because they are enamored of him or mistake him for a god, but only because they want to get from him the technique mastered. Therefore some spiritual masters carefully hide the austerities and pretend that their developed power was natural. Some who are even more intelligent simply perform the austerities in a previous life and carefully isolate themselves in that life, so they can keep the power in reservation. Then they pass from the body in which they performed the austerities and take a new body through which the austerity becomes manifest. The austerity or the result of it is stored in the subtle body. When the new gross body is acquired the austerity is displayed as a mystic or divine power. Then the spiritual master flashes himself on human society and attracts a large following.

Since many human beings are naturally superstitious, naturally simple-minded, they follow such a leader for better or worse, all depending on their affinity to the doctrine he propagates and the disciplinary processes he favors. Such is this particular ruse.

If the spiritual master passed away after accumulation of much austerity he develops a reserve of spiritual power, enabling him to control certain social conditions. When he takes a new body he may, by the acquired power, perform miracles here and there. Or he might give flashes of enlightenment to disciples. This is called empowered transmission (shaktipat). Many spiritual masters decry this energy transfer as hocus pocus, magic tricks, but it is true that some spiritual masters have the power to do this.

Those who decry it are either envious because they do not have such power cultivated or they simply use a propaganda tactic to attract people to their own camp. Shaktipat power, mystic power of a spiritual master, power that is reserved in his subtle body from past austerity, is factual. Its misuse or proper use is also factual.

The Bhagavad Gītā gave the example of such transcendental transfer when Arjuna was directly shown the Universal Form. Arjuna's hair stood on end. He began to respect Lord Krishna from every conceivable direction. Krishna as the Absolute Person exhibited mystic power effortlessly without performance of austerity, but the ordinary spiritual master acquires potency by penance in the present or past life.

The problem with such development of mystic power is its misuse. The misuse does not deny the power; it merely shows us that the power does exist and that once acquired it is difficult to control. A spiritual master who has such power and who consistently suppresses it or uses it in a way which brings no recognition, is a greater personality than one who flashes it. As such the criticism of its glaring use in human society is justified, since by such usage, people are usually misled and the user comes to certain ruination.

The development of spiritual power is of special interest to serious seekers since in such development vital techniques are used. Therefore if the spiritual master hides the process of his development, he cheats the followers. For instance, a seeker practiced austerities in the Himalayan Mountains in India. After ten years he got a visa and came to the United States. He attracted followers. He advocated a certain process, but he did not reveal the techniques of austerity. He simply began the authorized or unauthorized doctrine which he adapted to suit the needs of disciples. These disciples, being naive, never stop to consider the austerities performed by the teacher. They feel that they will become like him, even though they do not know the techniques he used. The serious seekers, however, pry into the background of the spiritual master. If they are successful they learn the technique.

Some spiritual masters simply do not discuss techniques of austerity because they have no faith in humanity. They feel that the average human being cannot perform such austerities and therefore, in their view, time would be wasted describing penances. Others, who performed the austerities in previous lives, do not remember the austerities in detail and feel in part that their powers are naturally endowed.

However, there is the legend of Brahma, the cosmic creative god. He performed austerities of introspective penance, the highest austerities for the conservation of personal power and communication with higher-ups. His sons, who were great yogins, suspected that he had a secret technique of communication with someone greater who was in another dimension. They sent Narad, their youngest brother, to question him. Narad approached Brahma privately and asked for the truth in the matter, stating that Brahma was suspect, because he performed mental austerities in strict discipline and because he tried to contact someone who was in another dimension.

The degree of austerities Brahma performed was unknown to his sons. The techniques he used were so subtle that it took them some time to even realize that he performed them. Thus he carefully hid the process and posed as being naturally powerful but his sons began to realize that he took power from a greater person than himself. After being confronted by Narada, Brahma admitted that he was not The Absolute Person and that he communicated with that divinity who existed in another dimension.

Some spiritual masters are so clever that they admit a greater person than themselves while presenting themselves as sole agent, total representative, and only person through which one may serve the Supreme. In other words, they bar the way between their disciples and their own master or God. This is another trick of the trade in the technique of being a spiritual master. On one hand these teachers speak greatly and faithfully about the teacher or Deity, and on the other hand they teach in such a way as to discourage or block any person who might want to speak or communicate directly with the superior.

Chapter 3

Advancement of

a Spiritual Master

Usually an empowered spiritual master brings himself to a certain level of advancement or he is brought to that level by his teacher and then he opens a mission to teach. As soon as this occurs, he attracts followers but his personal advancement may be neglected. He becomes occupied with problems of disciples, his image to the public, the reputation, the prestige and any impure desires which might surface due to his lack of continuing austerities.

There are regulative principles or a code of conduct, but in either case, the spiritual master will struggle to maintain these principles after he begins accepting disciples. The impurity of disciples affects him. If he wants world supremacy, if he wants to be known as a world teacher, if he thinks that his process is the highest or that he is especially empowered to save humanity, then he may sacrifice some principles.

Besides the code of conduct, the spiritual master will have to find time to continue his austerities. If he cannot find time, due to preoccupation with disciples, lectures, meetings, and showmanship, then his progress will surely decline. However his spiritual progress and his acquirement of fame in human society are two different aspects.

Usually as the spiritual progress declines, the fame increases until the point is reached where the fame begins to decline and the mission of the teacher falters. At that point the teacher begins to realize that something is amiss, but instead of retracing his steps and implementing corrective measures, he endeavors with more zeal to expand the mission.

Some rules are universally applicable to all spiritual teachers. It is common to spiritual development of all spiritual societies. It is common because the human being is a common factor in each case and the improvement of the human being takes place under certain standard conditions only.

For the spiritual master full purity means both internal and external control. Partial purity means much external control and little internal restraint. And it depends on the audience. If a spiritual master faces undisciplined persons, he will be required to hold up a poor standard of morality while before a well-informed group of cultured people he will have to promote something higher if he is to be accepted as an authority. Thus it is flexible. Ultimately however, spiritual advancement is inflexible.

In practice the spiritual master disregards the ultimate consideration and deals with the practical application. The more permissive the audience, the more the spiritual master can relax, enjoy and flaunt his advancement. The more cultured the audience is, the more particular and attentive he must be. We will now consider the universal applicable regulations which apply to any spiritual master, minister or religious leader.

Giving up the general path

This means conventional religious practices. For purification and success in austerity, one must give up the general path followed by humanity. If one does not do this one cannot become a great spiritual master. We have already proven this point by stating that the empowered spiritual master or his agent performed some austerity in the present or past life and then returned to human society. Leaving the general path is the stage of performing these austerities. When a person leaves the general path of religion or traditional recommended way, he embarks on the high road where he makes solid spiritual progress through performance of austerities. This course, however, does not necessarily clear the person of bad motivations, but it does cause conservation of psychological power which creates an automatic increase in psychic perception and mystic power.

Essentially this means that by such austerities one may or may not become purified of bad motives. A person may perform the standard austerities in yoga practice but his bad motive may remain intact. When he gets the desired power, he returns to human society and institutes a reign of terror. We also see in modern times that some political people are arrested by their opponents, put into a prison cell for many years or are exiled from the homeland and then years after they return with greater power after performing some type of austerity. At that time their bad motivation may remain intact but they trick the people, seize control of the country and create a constitution which says that they are the authorized ruler for their life time.

There are also positive examples. In one legend, the boy Dhruva had a motive to become the greatest ruler in this universe but after performing the advanced yoga disciplines and assuming a spiritual body and seeing the deity, his attitude changed. In other words, he was purified in the course of austerities. The result all depends on how the austerities are performed and who directs one in the disciplines.

Generally speaking no one can become liberated by following a general path of religion. It is simply talk when any leader states that one will be completely liberated. The general path is a diluted process that does not have the strength to vanquish our affinity to material nature. It merely serves to keep us morally-inclined in a specific way and gives us a sense of confidence to follow an authorized process. In any case, one must judge by the attained result. These results must be internal as well as external. If it is external only, it is certainly a farce. If it gives partial success on the internal plane then it falls short of success.

Once the spiritual master ceases an isolated life he returns to the human society and adopts a general path. He does this because he does not want to frighten anyone. To gather a large following one must make concessions, otherwise many people will run away. Therefore the teacher adopts a common process and the easier the process the more likely he is to attract followers. If he sticks to hard core austerities, he will have very few followers.

Salvation

Salvation is attained by endeavor and by divine grace. A righteous lifestyle is the foundation from which one may attain salvation. Therefore, in the stage of isolated austerities described above, the spiritual master has to discover those direct paths to salvation through which he gains actual experiences of the transcendental world. He not only hears of such a world but actually sees it and sees the divine beings there. To do this, he must assume possession of a spiritual body with spiritual eyes and other required senses. That is salvation. Merely hearing what someone says and not experiencing the reality behind the description, is not salvation but many followers are content with hearing and become convinced by the authority that they get the full experience through hearing.

Diet control

While one is in seclusion practicing austerities to become a spiritual master, one must control diet. One must reduce eating. This means that when one returns to human society, one must switch back; otherwise people will be frightened by the adversity. Nearly every human being likes high protein foods. The spiritual master must switch back to human habit. When he returns to human society with mystic power or with charismatic influence and missionary spirit, he may refrain from eating fish, eggs or meat, but still he has to agree to eat some type of rich food even if it is rich vegetarian meals. As far as the Christian ministers are concerned, they are not restricted to vegetarian foods. Still they have restrictions. Some of them do not eat pork. Some of them do not eat flesh of wild animals. Some of them make sure that the meat comes from animals which are killed by cutting the jugular vein so that the blood is drained from the body. Of course, from a vegetarian view point, that is sophisticated barbarism. Some seekers eat no flesh. Some eat eggs but no other type of meat product. It varies.

Eating frugally is required in isolation but once the spiritual master returns to human society to become recognized, he will invariably adopt richer foods. It is the law of nature that if one associates with many people one has to make adjustments. For this reason we find that some spiritual teachers assert a right to seclusion. They remain isolated for weeks, months, or years, just to recover themselves from the effects of having followers.

Seclusion

The purpose of seclusion is to clear off contamination which comes from disciples and members of the public, and to allow the authority to recover his focus on self-purity.

One trick of gurus is to pretend that they are not affected by mixing with others. This is a necessary pretense since no one would acclaim an authority who falls apart when he mixes with the public.

The procedure is this: The spiritual master carries with him a reserve energy which protects him from being lowered on psychological plane. The protection, however, is only partial. If the authority remains in contact with lowering influences for an extended period, he will be degraded no matter what he says. A cup of water cannot remain sterile if a teaspoon of bacteria is mixed with it. A lake is not contaminated if that amount of bacteria is added to it. But if one keeps adding more and more teaspoons, sooner or later the lake will be imperiled.

Thus if a spiritual master does not go into seclusion time after time, according to the degree of contamination, he will be degraded. The pretense of freedom from contamination is just fine, but a spiritual master must protect himself on the psychological level or his psychological energies will sink to a lower plane.

Nonviolence

Saintliness means to adhere to a complicated mesh of nonviolent values. How is that possible when even to breathe air one kills microbes?

Even vegetarians can only make a partial claim to non-violence. The question is: To what degree is a saint non-violent? No one can use a material body which is not engaged in violence to a living creature, no matter how microscopic that creature may be.

When a spiritual master mixes with others, he automatically imperils his non-violent vows if the said persons are involved in a lifestyle which has more violent content than his own. The danger of violence is not the violence itself but the resentment which one must process and which results from the violence. When a violent act is committed for any purpose, resentment energies are released. These must be processed by the individuals concerned, by both the victims and the assailants. It does not matter what justifiable or unjustifiable reason is applied.

To give us some idea of the extent of liabilities and to explain the Supreme Being's objections, Krishna made a revealing statement in the Bhagavad Gītā:

The Lord does not create the means of action, nor the actions of the creatures, nor the action-consequence cycle. But the inherent nature causes this.

The Almighty God does not receive from anyone, an evil consequence nor a good reaction. The knowledge of this is shrouded by ignorance through which the people are deluded. (Bhagavad Gītā 5.14-15)

This means that the spiritual master, like everyone else, must deal with the results of his interactions with others. If resentments come from creatures whose bodies he uses for food, he must deal with that himself, even though it is nice to think that God will compensate the followers.

Truthfulness

This is two-fold, being simple and complex. For a neophyte religionist this is simple. For an advanced soul this is complex. The ordinary person worries about social dealings. The advanced person worries about the earthly, astral, causal and spiritual relationships. Since the ordinary one is concerned with the physical only, his truthfulness has to do with refraining from telling untruths. However, even for him with this small aim, there is some difficulty.

Telling untruth is not merely a matter of taking a vow against falsehood. If a man is in an awkward situation, he will more than likely assume a dishonest attitude. Therefore, to avoid untruth, one must cultivate the habit of truthfulness as well as learn to keep oneself in very simple circumstances. Otherwise no matter how much one promises, one will be untruthful. This is nature. It is not merely a matter of our determination. Human determination is only effective when it is facilitated by destiny which is much more powerful than any human vow, and which could force the most upright man into a corner where he is forced to act in a contrary way.

For basic truthfulness, one cannot be successful unless one lives very simply, is satisfied, is very skilled at maintaining the things he needs for daily living and is content to cooperate with destiny in all circumstances. Unless one is an easy going, able person, one cannot maintain full truthfulness.

Christianity is a religion which focuses on social truthfulness but actually such truthfulness in incomplete. If, for instance, a Christian merchant is asked if he lies on a daily basis, he might say no, but if he is asked further to explain his profit margin he will be hesitant to answer. In other words, his livelihood is full of lies and he cannot avoid speaking untruth. Total honesty is impractical for such a person. Even though he resolved not to lie, his way of life requires a minimal dishonesty.

While the ordinary man is concerned with dishonesty on the physical level, the more advanced transcendentalist is concerned with truth on the subtle planes. This begins a review of one's mental and emotional complexities, through which one connives within the mind. One may speak truthfully on the physical side and feel differently on the subtle plane. Or one many act graciously on the physical side and act viciously on the subtle planes. Those who are advanced want to reform their natures thoroughly on all levels, because unless one is reformed even on the subtle planes, one cannot associate fully with divinity.

In the struggle for existence and livelihood there is a need for plotting and scheming, but if we can get out of this struggle, the need will go away and the defense mechanism that drives us into insecurity will drop off.

Spiritual masters usually connive but they hide the dishonesty very carefully. This is one of the tricks of the trade of being a guru. I once knew a spiritual master who would say one thing and mean the contrary. His close associates usually knew when he was dishonest, but they enjoyed it, feeling that their spiritual master outsmarted opponents and effectively advanced the mission. Eventually, however, he was ruined. Circumstances upturned his destiny and caused disgrace. In public meetings, he would say, "In our society, we leave everything in the open. Nothing is done privately that we do not reveal. We have nothing to hide. We are honest. Our dealings are the best. Which other spiritual society is as pure?" However, he lied considerably because much of the activities were criminal. Later when this was shown, many people left the group. Some of the close associates became distrustful of him.

The material world is so designed that a certain amount of dishonesty is required. The only way to avoid this is to reduce desires and bring one's nature under control. The more one desires, the more one indulges in schemes.

Desires, good or bad ones, mean fulfillment of the same, and for fulfillment there must be pressure applied on material nature and on fellow creatures. If material nature does not cooperate and if associates do not assist, we are forced to pressure them or give up the desires. If we do not give up the desires, we have to apply pressure and that causes exploitation, which causes resentment, which means defense. Defense implies violence and dishonesty. It does not matter if one desires something good or bad; even the good desires require a certain amount of violence.

Those spiritual teachers who have grand desires to spread their religion all over the world, will have to engage in dishonesty. Some of these teachers carefully and politely describe their untruth as useful propaganda.

For instance, if a spiritual master feels that his religious doctrine is not being taken seriously by the public, he may create a slogan to suit public needs and to attract the public by a promise of indulgence. To make it sound good, he will have to endorse that enjoyment as being a legitimate part of the religion. He might say that the indulgence will give salvation. Actually it will give no such thing, but once he convinces himself that he must fulfill the desire, he will develop the required dishonesty and force of power to tell people the untruth convincingly. Some human beings, naive as they are, will believe him and follow him to their dismay.

A spiritual master who wants a big mission and who does not have the natural facility must either acquire finances or give up the desire and stay humble in a corner as an unknown guru or minister. If he cannot detach himself from the desire, he may propagandize and influence rich and poor people to contribute money to his mission. If after expressing such an influence, sufficient money does not materialize, he will have to do something dishonest or encourage his disciple to do so or make disciples of dishonest people who require no impetus for viciousness. If he fails at this and realizes the deviation, he will scale down his grand desires for the world's salvation

If, for instance, a spiritual master comes from India and comes to America, he might find that Christianity is so rooted in the United States that he cannot easily make converts. He might find that in India, people easily give donations while in the West, the majority of businessmen give to their favorite charity or Christian church only. So what should he do to get large donations from big businesses?

If after experiencing this, he still cannot scale down his plans, he will have to engage in some type of immoral activities and cover his tracks from legal authorities, or face a jail term. The covering of tracks of a spiritual master means that he does not directly engage in any questionable activity. He keeps himself publicly clean, while secretly allowing his followers to do something illicit.

Eventually, however, law enforcement officials may begin questioning his organization. Once the government people grant him non-profit status as a religious organization with tax exemption privileges, they will inevitably check on him. When they see his material successes, they will ask for an explanation. At that point, the spiritual master will scramble for cover to avoid prosecution. Therefore, a spiritual master will have to scheme if he is to manifest his desires under such unfavorable conditions.

Another aspect is that even though the spiritual master might not commit any immoral activities, he will still be implicated if he is indirectly benefitting from anyone else's criminal activity. He may excuse himself by saying that the money is used for God and not for himself. In that way he will silence his conscience and continue in an immoral way, at least until he is pressured by time and destiny to stop this behavior. In addition, the disciples who engage in such immoral acts will eventually become disheartened, especially if they are caught by the police and jailed or intimidated accordingly. Then they will ask themselves if it was worth the consequence.

This writer once knew a man who used dishonest methods to raise money for the missionary activities of his spiritual master. The disciple raised thousands of dollars in that way and gave it to the spiritual master for printing books, constructing large buildings and other related missionary activities. Eventually he stopped this. When he met the writer, he explained, "Yes, it is a fact that I used to go to India frequently. I would go there with television sets from Hong Kong or Japan and I would sell at a profit but sometimes I would, in return, buy some other items. The secret was this: We used to buy narcotics to bring to the United States and England, where we would sell the hashish or opium for a huge profit to drug dealers. To cover our activities, we pretended to be traders, who carried one item into a country, sold it there and then bought a local product and took it to the home port. In this way we pretended to be a legitimate trading firm but underneath we were drug dealers.

"I was caught twice. Once when I returned to England, I was caught and jailed. My wife took care of me. She visited the prison. In the mean time, the spiritual master to whom I gave most of the profit, disowned me. He could not afford to tarnish his public image. After two jail terms, I ceased. I reconsidered and understood that he did not care about me. He wanted the money but not the risk. He protected himself from being directly involved. I suffered. He avoided hassles with the law."

Some spiritual masters protect themselves by not knowing how the disciples acquire money. They do this by asking one of the disciples to establish a mission. In other words, if the mission is established in the name of the spiritual master directly and if by the view of the government people, there are discrepancies in fund-raising, the spiritual master might be arrested. To avoid this some spiritual masters make sure that their names are not on any legal charters or trusts. In that case if anything questionable comes up they cannot be taken to court.

Some spiritual masters are even more clever, however. They set up headquarters in a foreign country like India. Since they are unable to raise hard currency in India, they make disciples in the developed countries. These disciples acquire money in the foreign countries either legally or illegally and send it to their spiritual master, who establishes himself abroad. In some cases the situation is reversed where a spiritual master in the United States will send disciples to New Zealand, Japan, Hong Kong, Malaysia, Australia , Brazil or some such place to acquire finances. These disciples go there, invent some dishonest means and raise large sums of money, then get it to their spiritual master in one way or the other so that he can show his glory and fulfill his missionary desires.

Another method used by some spiritual masters who are even more devious, is to remain at their headquarters in a developed country and raise money illegally but carefully have this money shown to government authorities as legal money. There are numerous ways of doing this but one favorite method is to find sympathetic wealthy patrons who could underwrite such money by pretending to donate the illegally gained funds. This is how it works: The spiritual master gets some disciples to acquire and sell narcotics or some other questionable item, even something such as tricking a bank into giving a loan by creating false collateral. Once the money is acquired the spiritual master consults with rich followers. He convinces the wealthy person to give him a statement saying that a certain large sum of money was donated. This statement is shown to the Income Tax Authorities and in that way the illegally raised money is hidden under the guise of a hefty donation from a well wisher.

All these activities are part of untruth. They tarnish a spiritual master. Eventually they ruin his mission. These habits corrupt a guru. They are a violation of saintly principles. They are only supportive of uncontrollable passionate desires which pass as religious activities.

Refraining from theft

Refraining from theft is one of the moral principles. In some spiritual societies such a thing as refraining from theft is not mentioned. In others it is mentioned as an irrelevant quality. The spiritual leader assures the followers that in this time, in such a weakened condition, God adjusted these difficult principles and substituted easier ones which will give one the same salvation gained before by people who lived honestly in better times. Such statements, however, are oversimplifications. They are in fact, distortions of the truth.

Like untruth, stealing is a bad quality and it degrades the actor. Therefore, it cannot be dismissed. It is a bad trait for people on the spiritual path. Once years ago, this writer had a feeling to find an expensive chair. At first I thought that I might need such a chair but later I realized that I did not since it was never my habit to live in luxury. I was always satisfied with simple things. However, being pressed by the desire, I went out and found a chair at the back of a building. The chair was not discarded but it was lying at the back of the building after the building was closed for the day's business. I took the chair and returned home with it. While I journeyed home, I had a feeling that I had just stolen someone's chair. I began to analyze my motive, asking if I wanted someone to steal a similar item from me in the future and if I would be satisfied with such a sudden loss of property. Gradually, after much deliberation and psychic tracking, I realized that I was influenced by a departed spiritual master. He inspired the theft because he wanted his subtle body to sit on that expensive chair. He inspired me to place his picture on the chair. He used to visit the writer in his astral form and he would sit on the chair. After a while, I began to plead with him about it. I said, "You are a spiritual master. When you left your body you were famous. Now you are still famous. Why did you take advantage when I was off guard and influence me to steal this chair? Suppose I was arrested. Or suppose there is a reaction in the future as there are always reactions in material nature. Which of us will absorb the reaction? Who is responsible?"

And of course, he did not answer. So, in that case, I stole something to please a spiritual master. But that is a violation of regulative principles and unlike others, my conscience ached and never allowed me to rationalize it away. There definitely will be a reaction for it, because the spiritual master should get things honestly. Why should he steal an ornate chair just to present himself as an authority over everyone? Why should he, as a transcendentalist, be so attached to sitting on a decorated chair that he would imperil a disciple by influencing the disciple to steal something which would contravene godly principles?

So long as there are exorbitant desires and rampant passion in the spiritual master he will have to take to immoral practices in one way or another to adjust his destiny so that he can fulfill plans. It is a law of psychological nature. One takes birth on the basis of past pious or impious activities in conjunction with the reasonable desires that can be easily fulfilled by destiny within a certain historic phase. If one increases the desires, destiny may remain as it is and then one must pressure destiny which means violence and criminality. If one has a reputation and image to protect, one will have to protect oneself and sacrifice others by influencing them to do illicit acts which may or may not land them in trouble in short range but which in the long range, will convert negatively.

Some spiritual masters, however, assure followers that they will be protected by God and guru. This is mostly talk. I remember years ago, a famous sannyasi spiritual master from India had a general secretary who was very popular but actually the general secretary was a narcotic dealer. He got his position as general secretary because of the criminally-acquired money he used to give the spiritual master. In any case, time demanded that the spiritual master depart from his body. There was a power struggle in the society. Some disciples emerged victorious as staunch leaders. This particular general secretary then had to become secretary of one of his god brothers. He did not like the idea but he complied because his spiritual master was departed. He still wanted to identify himself strongly with the society.

Gradually he became disgusted with the new leaders who were his god brothers, fellow disciples of his guru. He said to me, "These men treat me as a newcomer, as one of their disciples. They demand the same service of me that I rendered to our guru. I do not know how long I will be able to function among them." In any case, under pressure from a prominent leader, one of his god brothers, he went to India and tried to smuggle a large quantity of narcotics into a developed country. Unfortunately he was arrested, tried and imprisoned. After that he left the society in disgust.

The promise that he would be protected by God and guru fell through. He was arrested, tried and served a jail term. When released he avoided the spiritual society and tried to expose the leaders.

Years ago, we had a similar experience where a spiritual master of repute practically ordered the writer to get money by hook or crook, disregarding all moral ways of acquiring funds. He unquestionably followed in the footsteps of his spiritual master and because his spiritual master did that to him, he demanded that his disciples render a similar service. He created a list of names of important disciples and put a sum of money in thousands of dollars beside each name. He distributed the list to the disciples concerned, telling each to acquire that money in two months to finish a project.

This is a subtle trick played by some spiritual masters to create a competitive attitude among followers. Some disciples will get the money required because they know how to raise money by honest or dishonest means, by appealing for donations or by outright trickery. Some may have wealthy parents. Some operate business concerns. Others may be criminals or drug dealers or have some type of questionable activity for acquiring funds. Therefore these particular ones will raise the allotted sum. The spiritual master is confident of this. However, he knows that the total money they will raise will not be sufficient for his needs. Therefore, he will create a pressure on others to get the remaining amount, knowing fully well that others have poor parents, have no business acumen, and have no criminal habits. He will use the tactic of presenting their names publicly on a sheet to intimidate them. This would be effective on persons with a weak conscience. In other words, some who are not thieves will start stealing. Some who are not dope pushers might go out and try their hands at it. That is the way it works. It so happened that on the particular occasion the conscience of the author was strong. I effectively resisted even though I absorbed resentments from the spiritual master and from the other prominent members who usually raise large sums of money in one way or another.

Some disciples who were already doing illegal things and who enjoyed these activities, went out and did more. A few were caught and jailed. Others indulged in bank fraud. One particular man got some money from a bank and then invested the money in the purchase of narcotics to reap a huge profit. All the while, he thought he was doing the right thing. He thought that he did it for God and guru. The guru shared the same belief. This means that one must be careful with spiritual masters, especially those who are fame-crazy and who would do anything or make their followers do any and everything to fulfill missionary plans. To be a missionary is one thing. To perform anti-religious activities to further the missionary spirit is an entirely different matter. It is just like wanting heat and pouring water over the fire from which the heat emanates.

The sad fact is that one must accept a spiritual master if one wants to progress spiritually. There is no alternative. In most cases, one may take a vice-prone authority, because such a person may have a technique or process one badly needs for advancement. One should know how to deal with an authority without becoming victimized by him.

Possessing basic needs

To possess only what is necessary and to live simply is easy for a disciple who is isolated but it is difficult for a spiritual master who mixes with the public. Once a spiritual master opens missionary societies, he enters a deadly trap from which he may not extricate himself even at the time of death. The trap is that he will have to deal with the energies of disciples. Some disciples might have spiritually-resistant natures, vice-prone natures and uninhibited sensory natures. Thus the spiritual master may become affected. If one checks closely, one will find that as soon as a spiritual master becomes famous, he may develop an attachment to opulence. Some spiritual masters might have been poor holy men in India but upon migrating to the United States or United Kingdom and getting many disciples, all of a sudden they begin wearing gold, diamond rings, wrist watches, fancy clothing and living in large palatial houses, sitting on expensive chairs, riding in sedans and limousines. All of a sudden they begin to possess more than necessary. After a few years, the income tax authorities check on their finances and they cry in defiance, "They attack me!" Sometimes they flee to an undeveloped country to escape the scrutiny.

If we can find a spiritual master who is famous and who still remains simple with no gold, no diamonds, no mansion, only living simply and allowing God alone to be glorified by using donations for God's glory, leaving himself aside, then we have found a most unusual authority. Where is that person? Which society can claim such a leader? Who is so simple and humble?

After all, we follow a spiritual master because we admire him. On occasion we follow a spiritual master because we envy and admire him simultaneously. That means that unless he does something we may envy, we will not follow him. Unless he attained the glory we long for, we will not serve him. Which of us could follow a spiritual master who does not flash opulence, fancy food, limousines, jet plane rides and the like? Which of us is so pure? This is why we have to take the spiritual master as he is, despite real or imagined faults. We must get some benefit from him regardless, without ruining ourselves in his association.

Accepting only what is necessary

Unless one is frugal in needs and subdued in desires, one cannot accept only what is necessary. When a spiritual master begins a preaching mission or decides that he is going to fulfill his mission to save the world or to assist God in saving the world, he runs a high risk of confusing personal desires for world supremacy with God's desires for man's salvation. His tendency will be to possess more than is necessary and to pass it off as acts which are necessary in the service of God and humanity.

Unless one is fully purified before one takes the post of guru or before advertising oneself as a special servant or agent of God, one is bound to make mistakes. According to some processes the spiritual master becomes purer as he advances but this does not happen if the spiritual master becomes lazy in personal practice. He becomes slack in watching his desires. He is carried away, grasping for more than he needs. In the confusion he publicizes the idea that whatever he does is not for himself but for God.

One should become a spiritual master if one is purged of the rulership tendency. Many spiritual masters are part-time saints. Therefore, when they become established as founders of a particular society, their rulership tendency comes into play. In these societies which they establish, they become like kings with great autocratic power. Along with the rulership qualities, there are rulership desires. When these surface and the spiritual master plays them out with disciples, he is bound to pass off many personal needs as being God-sanctioned or God-inspired. Thus he will take great risks, feeling that God will protect. Then there might be a disaster which puts him into an awkward position from which he cannot extricate himself.

There is a legend of King Vishwa who wanted to be rated as a saint. He was rejected by Saint Vasish. Vishwa was determined. After many years, he attained the saint status. He endeavored for purification before he established himself as a holy man. He did not take the risk to open a mission while developing himself as he went along. Vishwa took years to develop himself. As he reformed he used to check with Saint Vasish and others, to get their view about his progress. Repeatedly he was told that he was below the standard until at last, he was accepted when his nature changed completely and permanently into that of a saint. Nowadays, however, many spiritual masters, assume that they will progress as their societies develop but their impure nature fosters misjudgment and miscalculation.

To possess only what is necessary is not a mental plan. One may want to be like that but if one's nature is passionate, one will take more than required. Therefore, one must first be purified in nature before one can master this quality. In other words, if we do not change internally and if we do not become purified completely of lower modes, we are bound to possess more than necessary and to grasp for things that will hurt us in the long run.

Material nature is not concerned with our sense of conviction or belief or with our power of persuasion through which we influence others. Nature is concerned with our tendency and routine modes of operation through which She lowers or elevates us. Until the spiritual master moves entirely out of the lower modes, there is no question of purity in desire every step of the way.

Some spiritual masters issue the idea that since their mission is blooming, since it is increasing, since they are getting more and more publicity and acceptance that they are empowered by God and that their mission is solid. But a few years later when the mission begins to shrink and followers start to dwindle, they cannot explain the circumstances. This implies that the expansion and contraction of a spiritual society is not an accurate way to judge progress of the mission. Movements of destiny are there, in the form of increasing or decreasing the fulfillment of desires. These are not necessarily divinely-approved, even though they are certainly divinely-allowed.

Unless a spiritual master is saintly in the truest sense, fully purified before he starts a mission, there is every chance that he will use the mission which is established in God's name, for his own glorification, to fulfill his desire to rule over others. As such many people will be fooled into thinking they are serving God when in fact they are merely fulfilling the teacher's gigantic greed for power and rulership. When a soldier gets an order to sacrifice his life in war, he may face enemy fire and be killed uselessly in a plan of the politicians. Similarly a disciple may sacrifice himself, commit criminal acts for a spiritual master who is power-drunk, power-crazy, being carried away by a wave of success.

Since we as disciples, we as persons trying for spiritual success, must deal with spiritual masters, we must learn to recognize when the authority confuses himself with God. We must learn to side step him on occasion without offending him and still be able to serve him and get the needed techniques we require from him.

There was a legend of Shukra who was not rated as a saint by many persons. In fact he was advanced and knowledgeable in psychic matters but he had bad motivation. He accepted many criminal and corrupt people as disciples because he wanted to be in a position to rule over others. In any case, Kach, a perceptive boy who was a disciple of a rival guru, took initiation from Shukra and served him for sometime, to get medical knowledge about reviving dead bodies. So it is like that. If the spiritual master is a power-hungry, popularity-crazed man and if he still thinks that he is divine, and if we need to get a technique from him, we should refrain from criticizing him. If I criticize the spiritual master, even mentally, the master may detect it and I may not get his cooperation. Thus the need for a technique which he pioneered might be frustrated.

After seeing or hearing about the fault of a spiritual master, someone might get disgusted and go away. This is mostly due to an idealistic misconception. The misconception is that the spiritual master should be perfect, especially if he indicates that he is. Still one must understand that every spiritual master has a human side and only in so far as the spiritual master can transcend his humanity can he be free of vicious dealings. Therefore the disciples, the seekers, have to be very intelligent and willing to overlook the bad nature.

In the material world, almost everything is upside down. Therefore one should not expect perfection even in the spiritual societies of worth. One should expect contrariness and be willing to work through a maze of illusions to accomplish the spiritual goals. After all, whatever particular disciplines were mastered by the teacher is known to him. If one needs the information or technique mastered by a particular teacher, one will have to serve him to get it. It is a matter of serving out the requirement with the least possible harm to oneself.

The quality we are discussing, the one of taking and accepting only for basic needs, is the very quality that will save or implicate a disciple who is following a fame-crazy spiritual master. Many fame-crazy gurus brand their desires as God's desires. The majority of their disciples will be like the spiritual master, in the sense that they will also have desires which they disguise as God's desires. Together with the Guru they enter into a false sense of security, thinking that God will take all liability for their acts. They may aspire for world supremacy only to find out years after, that their mission is frustrated and they are in legal difficulty. However, if one is sincere one can move among such spiritually-confused people and still benefit from them by learning any valid technique they may use. As I stated, whatever disciplines the spiritual master completed, can be learned from him if one is willing to serve as he demands. While serving, his bad qualities should be overlooked. One should keep away from his indulgent side. Many other disciples will be on the indulgent, confused side. One need not interfere with this.

By necessity, an army has two parts. The important part that will not be sacrificed and the unimportant part that will be committed in risky attacks. In army talk, the unimportant part is called cannon fodder. Fodder means feed and cannon means firing power. An experienced general, be he essentially a good or bad man, knows that the enemy will gain the upper hand from time to time. It is just the way of war. The general must sacrifice some men into the hands of the enemy. When he sends these men to the front lines, he knows that they will not return. The general thinks, "These men will not return. They will be killed. What can be done about it? In any case if they realize that they will be killed, they will go reluctantly. I will convince them of the victory. Once they are convinced they will bravely face the enemy."

In spiritual life, certain disciples of a popular spiritual master will be defeated and will not attain perfection in the particular life, but an intelligent disciple must take note of this and get whatever disciplines, techniques or processes he needs from the teacher, even if he knows well that the teacher and the careless disciples will fail in their mission.

The energy to possess more than required, comes from the energy that is not used to tighten one's austerity in spiritual life. As soon as the spiritual master or disciple relaxes from disciplines in austerity and further refinement of spiritual progress, they begin to possess more than necessary, because this is the law of nature. Usually in each spiritual group there is a stressed discipline and a neglected process. Hardly one group has a complete, well rounded combination of austerities. Each group usually tries to stress one or two austerities and neglect others, or stress one or two processes to the neglect of others.

For instance, if one joins a yoga group one may be deprived of the opportunity for ceremonial deity worship or chanting. Other groups stress chanting of the name of God and do nothing else but collect money on the side. Some other groups stress fire sacrifices. Some stress ceremonial worship and chanting simultaneously. Others stress yoga and chanting simultaneously. It all depends on the training of the spiritual master. Each group lays claim to a complete process for salvation. Each group states that it can save the whole human being and give him the ultimate aim of life, which is defined differently according to the doctrine.

Apart from this, each group may only stress part of their process to the neglect of other parts. A serious student must realize this and find out what is needed for spiritual advancement. It is said that only an accursed person jumps from one spiritual master to another or from one group to another, but if one can only get a partial method from a guru, one may go elsewhere to learn whatever else one might require to complete spiritual life.

Usually a spiritual master requires service and/or money. Most teachers do not part with techniques easily. They set up checks and balances, restrictions and screening processes to protect themselves from exploitation by disciples, who may take the process and then go elsewhere without giving services or finances. The preference of the spiritual master is that disciples will come, become convinced, stay on and serve for the rest of their lives. So if the spiritual master detects that one will take a process from him and go away, he will either deny discipleship or charge a high price, either in the form of money or services.

The writer can give a personal experience. Years ago, I approached a yoga teacher for some techniques in hatha yoga. Ultimately hatha yoga means controlling the life force and once that it is done, celibacy is achieved. However, the techniques are rarely divulged by the masters of the art. In any case, as providence would have it, I had to relocate before I could get the whole procedure. The teacher said that he, too, was relocating to the same country shortly. After about nine months he moved. When I saw him, he requested that I surrender fully to his mission. As a result my life was diverted. Gradually I got the technique he mastered but to my dismay this was not the whole discipline but only a minor part of it.

In another experience, I joined a kundalini yoga group. The spiritual master lived far away. The members only saw him once per year. In any case, after staying there for some time we only got part of the process. I held a full time job, contributed most of my salary and worked at the society's restaurant late at night. After working at my regular job, during the day I washed dishes under steam in addition to attending all exercise sessions in the wee hours of the morning. From that teacher we got another part of the process.

In yet another experience, I joined a spiritual community because I needed to learn the ceremonial worship procedures and the proper approach to studying books like the Bhagavad-Gītā. Again I had to pay dearly. In that case the spiritual master emphasized the collection of money, large sums of it. I had no money. I ended up cleaning the compound's toilets for over three years. Still, because I wanted the information and process and because the spiritual master suspected that I would not follow him blindly and become his enamored worshipper, he charged a high price in the form of menial service. I did it willingly. Gradually he was moved by the heart to show the process. So these are some rigors of spiritual life. When it gets right down to it, hardly a man goes to a spiritual master because he is looking for someone to worship. Many of the spiritual masters are looking for fans, for people who would advocate them and tell the world how great the guru is. Therefore one has to know what one wants from a spiritual master or spiritual society. One has to be willing to pay the price stipulated.

One should be honest with oneself and know one's motivation. For instance, those who are most loyal to a spiritual master might be his worst enemies or his greatest competitors. In some cases this is revealed when the spiritual master is disgraced or when he leaves his body and there is a struggle to gain control of his fame, property and doctrine. Even those who are the best at pretending that they are loyal to a particular group, might be more motivated against the spiritual master than anyone else.

The spiritual master is not free of motivation either, at least not in terms of using disciples to fulfill personal desires which have little to do with God or with the disciples' spiritual progress. Still that does not mean that we can progress without a guru or the structure of a spiritual society. One may need one or both.

The conflict or tug of war between the spiritual master and disciple is shown in the Bhagavad Gītā in the beginning of the discourse. In fact, the Bhagavad Gītā begins with Arjuna trying to convince Krishna to do exactly what Arjuna thinks should be done. In other words, the disciple wanted to influence the spiritual master to subordinate. And of course that did not work. Lord Krishna chastised Arjuna and then later, Arjuna apologized. He said:

Whatever was said impulsively, considering You as a friend, such as, "Hey, Krishna! Hey, family man of the Yadus! Hey, buddy!" was done by me through ignorance of Your majestic supernatural glory or even by affectionate familiarity.

And with intent to joke, You were disrespectfully treated, while playing, while on a couch, while sitting, while dining privately or even in public, O infallible Krishna. For that I ask forgiveness of You Who are boundless. (Bhagavad Gītā 11.41-42)

So it is like that—the disciple is loaded with motives and the master too. On the battlefield of Kurukshetra, the disciple wanted to use the spiritual master and the spiritual master wanted to use the disciple. When this was realized, Arjuna came to understand that he could not influence Krishna. If anything, he had to claim Krishna as the master. If I want something from a spiritual master I would have to take the role of a student or dependent.

Deep inside, Arjuna had a plan to convince his relatives to cooperate and reconcile. Arjuna came to the battlefield for a show of power, to intimidate his relatives into accepting a peace agreement. Krishna already tried for peace by talking to the opponents. They rejected it. Arjuna's self interest was fame, either as a classic warrior or as a general who made peace. He preferred the nice guy role. At the last minute his intention was to get Krishna to use mystic power to charm the opponents. But Krishna wanted to use the mystical power to frighten the living wits out of the opponents in such a way to make them realize that the war they desired would result in their defeat.

Thus, in dealing with a spiritual master, if we want something from him, just as Arjuna wanted mystic support, we have to do what the spiritual master says, even if it is unpalatable; just as the writer who wanted a ceremonial process and a pattern of disciplic succession and was required to clean toilets. A price must be paid.

So long as we are slack in performance of austerities we will acquire more than necessary. This applies to the spiritual master and the disciples. There is no alternative but to increase austerities if we want to avoid extravaganza.

Celibacy

Celibacy is a must in spiritual life but nowadays practically all the spiritual groups neglect it. Those who are concerned about it show a superficial concern in which one gets a reputation of celibacy merely by adopting a position as a monk or sannyasi without learning any real technique for sex restraint and sublimation of the sexual urge. Practically every group lays claim to their process as being capable of giving celibacy without any special technique for curbing the life force.

Total celibacy in purity is only possible by kundalini yoga. Each group says their process can yield celibacy even if they know nothing about the kundalini techniques. As a result, there are perverted monks or priests and power-crazy spiritual leaders, whose sex drive either comes out in child molestation, homosexuality, masturbation or heterosexual involvement. Each group makes a claim, "Follow our process and you will get everything else automatically." A disciple, however, should be intelligent enough to know exactly what he will or will not get from a particular process regardless of what the leader or the blind followers say.

There are various stages of celibacy. Celibacy begins in its most elementary stage as a mere desire or longing to be free of the sex urge. This is the desire for an urge-free adult body. In an infant's body, the sex urge is not there and in an adult's body complete celibacy means that the body produces sexual fluids and still the urge for gross contact is not there. If the urge is there and one cannot fulfill it, one will either suppress it, masturbate or express it with a partner. It is as simple as that.

The male human body is so designed that if the sexual fluids flow in the area near the seminal vesicle tube in the ampulla portion of the spermatic cord, the fluid has to pass out of the body because it can no longer absorb into the body.

If there is only an emotional or romantic stimulation, the subtle body will be motivated to make a contact in the astral world. This is a description of the conditions which face any person using a gross male body. It is not so much who you are but what sort of body you utilize. The limitations of the body make true celibacy impossible for those who do not curb the life force by kundalini yoga. But kundalini yoga is not the full process. It is only part of the process of spiritual perfection just as many other processes are only parts of the total way.

Pranayama or hatha yoga technique

Celibacy means efficient absorption of the semen into the body from within the ductus deferens tube which leads from the testes. Only a portion of the semen will be absorbed in that way if one does not use pranayama and hatha yoga techniques. Once there are lusty thoughts, the semen in the tube is affected and it flows in such a way that it cannot be absorbed into the blood stream. Then it must be expelled or must flow out through the penis. There is no question about it. It is not a matter of sentiment. It is the way the human male sex apparatus functions. If just a little fluid reaches near the seminal vesicle it causes an agitation and if much reaches and is not expelled, it causes a swelling and a pain in the tubes. It is just the way a male body operates. If one does not take up kundalini yoga either through hatha yoga or pranayama or through both, then one will have to be completely lust-free which implies that one will have to avoid all types of sexual attraction in this world and in the subtle world, in thought, word, and deed. Even then one's celibacy will still be partial only because the blood from which the semen is manufactured will be lusty.

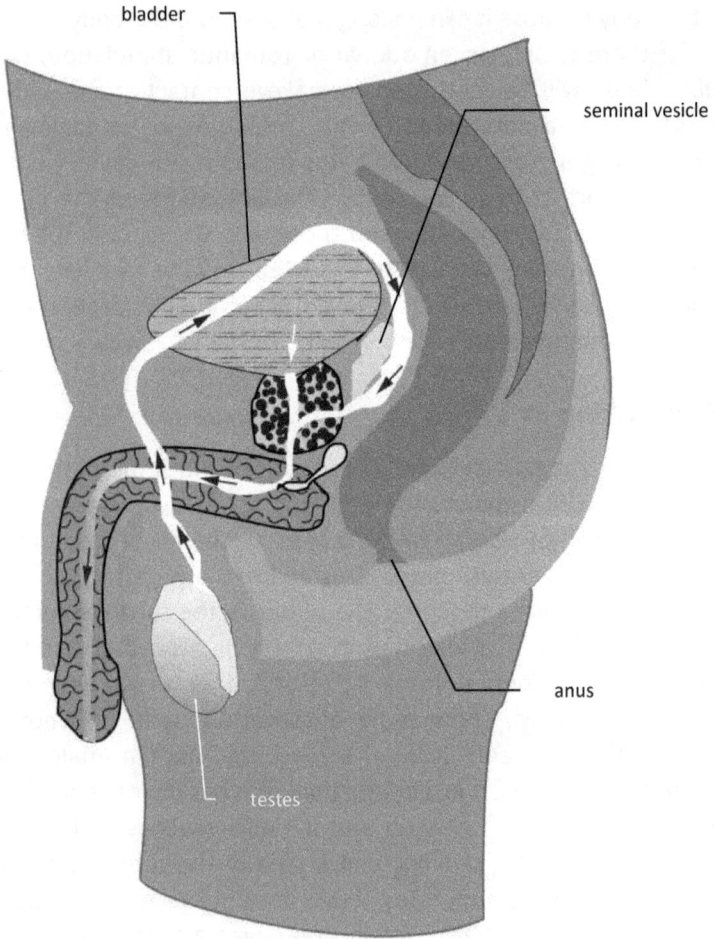

Arrows show emission path of sperm from testes through the left spermatic cord and into the penis.

Spiritual masters who are not perfect celibates will have to engage in some sort of sexual indulgence either grossly or subtly, or in both ways, not because of themselves but under bodily impulsion. The guru might have an idea of himself. He might have lofty aims and strong conviction, still the human body has certain limitations.

Another consideration is that one might find a celibate master, but he may have malicious intentions. That is another problem. Kashipu became celibate while performing austerities but he was ill-intended. There are numerous theists and devotees but so many of them are lax in austerity, being far away from celibacy. One cannot learn celibacy from a person with an indulgent body. It is not unusual to hear a lecture by a sannyasi monk who strongly condemns sexual indulgence and who is actively involved in homosexual practice.

Austerity

Austerity is a very broad term which includes any type of effective discipline which controls the unruly senses and saves the soul from becoming a total or partial stooge to the senses. Sanat, an ancient ascetic, gave a hint when he instructed Prithu on the effects of the uncontrolled senses. He said that the senses are like gigantic grass straws, and the self is comparable to a lake. If the giant grass straws are allowed to grow near the lake, they will eventually draw all reserve water. That is exactly what occurs if we allow ourselves to be stooges of the senses. So long as the senses are allowed to trigger the mind to act, the soul will be exploited and its reserve energies will be expended.

Power over others

To gain power over others, either as a spiritual master, politician or merchant, one must perform austerity either in the present or past life. Once one attains the position one will relax to enjoy the status. As soon as one relaxes, the senses will dominate the psyche. This is why some spiritual masters fall down. First they perform austerity. Then they become famous. Then they relax to enjoy the fame. At this point, the senses begin to mash them up systematically until we, the ones who once admired them, publicized and envied them, begin to wonder how they became so degraded.

Cleanliness

Cleanliness is defined differently in different spiritual societies. Generally this means at least two baths per day, cleaning of the mouth, regularity of evacuation, grooming of the face and hair, along with neat and clean clothing. In the Christian tradition, the cleaning of clothes might be neglected. For instance, a Christian man might wear a suit (external jacket) all year long without washing it. Then after a year, he may dry-clean it. That is considered as cleanliness. However, to be considered clean in some Vedic societies, one has to wash used clothing on a daily basis. Some Vedic groups are only concerned with outer bodily appearance and the cleanliness that involves. Others neglect the outside of the body or maintain it and also stress internal cleanliness of the lungs, intestinal tract and blood stream. This is when hatha yoga and pranayama are applied.

Doctrine/Belief

In developed countries, many religions spring up. Each group has its doctrine and belief. There are composite religions which are mixed, being in part Christianity, in part Hinduism, in part Buddhist and in part innovation. Each of these systems proclaims itself. In any case, it all depends on the individual needs. Seekers usually drift from one group to another, on and on, trying to find something that removes all delusion, banishes all unhappiness and brings instant and permanent enlightenment.

Worship of the Supreme

Worship of a Supreme Person is not always required. Some spiritual societies avoid worship of the Supreme Person. They substitute worship of something else like a book or a human teacher, the individual seeker himself, or a process of meditation or humanity or a conception of the sum-total reality as it is conceived by a certain leader. In each case, some objective focus or abstraction is used.

Silence

Silence is defined differently among various spiritual groups and has low priority in some. In fact in some groups silence is outlawed. While in meditation groups silence is appreciated, in groups which use singing, chanting or listening to music and special sounds, silence may be considered as negative.

Some spiritual masters extol silence and it is desired for those who want to reach samadhi high-dimension perception states. It is discouraged in some groups which consider the uttering of sacred sounds to be the best discipline.

Yogic postures

Postures can facilitate spiritual practice. In modern society, people are accustomed to the comfort of luxurious chairs and couches. On the mental level, one feels that it is only necessary to wish for spiritual life and to engage the mind and emotions and one does not feel a need to curb the material body. Therefore one hesitates to follow a doctrine which advocates purity of the body. However, most systems which depend only on wishing and thinking are incomplete systems, since the gross body affects the subtle one which affects the attitude of the person concerned.

Control of the vital air

This is the control of the subtle energy through control of the breath intake. Essentially this concerns two parts of the psyche, the lower part of the physical body beginning at the navel and going down the thigh, into the feet, and the purification of the subtle body. Material existence is more or less a process of conditioning or orientation to material life in a creature body. It is such a drain that the soul becomes involuntarily habituated to it for millions upon millions of years. The soul cannot release itself easily nor can it be freed by a guru's wishful thinking. The core-self should make a deliberate effort to get out. It should endeavor for freedom from lower dominance.

Depending on the level of their understanding, many spiritual masters think of or pretend that release from material existence is easily accomplished, but nothing is further from the truth. The soul is deeply engrained in a deadly, life-draining love affair with material nature. Its mental resistance does not stand for much in the face of its attachment.

The system of pranayama was practiced by many ancient yogis. Few became liberated without its practice. It has the capacity to free one from the lower modes and gives one the experience of the subtle body, the core-self, the vast spiritual level, the objective spiritual existence and divine people.

Withdrawing the mind from sense objects

This is internal detachment from the senses, accomplished by sensual detachment in concentration, meditation and routine life. In modern times, the definition changed considerably since human beings have multiple distractions. There are various recommended methods according to the various spiritual societies. One should find a process that works. In that quest, a seeker drifts from one spiritual group to the next looking for an effective procedure.

Each group claims that it has the perfect method but it is not so much the method as it is the various types of personalities. It depends on the particular addiction of sensual life of the personality. For instance, a friend who grew up listening to popular songs was attracted to a discipline which used sound to control the mind. Due to this attachment, he was not content in societies that did not stress sound focus. For another person, it might be a visual discipline. For yet another it might be emotional discipline or dietary discipline. Even though each spiritual master tries to spread a blanket over the whole of humanity to give a single process, people are essentially different and what advances one may do nothing for others.

A visual method is suitable to those who are attached to peering and visualization. A breathing process is given to those who are attached to air nutrition. A bodily process (postures) is given to those who are attached to the limbs and organs of the body. All these are linked to the mind and the objective is to get the mind under control by attracting and capturing its favorite sense organ. In some cases a person starts out with postures and progresses through that to another method. In other cases, one starts out by a chanting method and then finds it necessary to develop a visual discipline. Thus, there are variations according to the specific needs of the seeker.

Concentrating the mind on the heart

The central part of consciousness is the core of all psychic energies, the generation point of the psychic and super psychic force. By the yoga processes, one gradually attacks the various nexus of each part of the body. One finds the impediments to spiritual life and one systematically conquers the resistance, removing it entirely. One gradually becomes liberated in real terms as compared to an imaginative system that gives no actual experience but only fanciful hopes.

Many spiritual masters purport on the heavy-duty religious books from India and speak as if they know something about the systems of release mentioned, but unless they practiced these systems themselves, their knowledge is theoretical for the most. In such an analysis, their conclusions may be imperfect. They may belittle a system that has great value. They may underwrite a system that cannot deliver what it promises. Spiritual life means the individual decision to conquer attachment to material nature and get help in specific trouble areas that stall us. If we follow a system that does not give a result, we should be intelligent enough to realize the failure and find out from the scriptures how the ancient mystics practiced that system effectively. This is called following the path of the predecessors or the system of using proven methods of liberation.

Disciplic succession means more than finding a spiritual master who is an authorized successor from India. It also means to find any spiritual master or any process used by a perfected spiritual master in the past and to use that method for actual results in gaining release from the dreary and extended course of material existence. We were transmigrating in this miserable place for a long time past and we cannot assess the time spans of our mundane involvements.

Fixing the mind on one spot and lifting attention from lower chakras

This is the process of removing vital air from the lower parts of the gross and subtle body. Wherever the vital air goes, the consciousness follows. In spiritual life there is a struggle to get this vital force to cooperate. It is resistant, impulsive and offensive toward our will power. Unless it is deliberately purified and curbed, one cannot become free from its impulsive habits. This is why the ancient masters took the time to directly attack the life force, purify it and finally control it. They were not crazy. They did this because it is necessary for anyone to get full release.

When one can consistently concentrate the mind, he can release the life force from the lower part of the body. By getting full cooperation from the life force, one can shift the consciousness to higher dimensions.

We can start anywhere but ultimately, on this planet or on the next, in this life or in the next, we have to come to terms with impurities and make an all-out attack on negative subtle energies.

We are discussing the advancement of the spiritual master. Unless he is able to maintain advancement he will regress. This does not mean that he will not be successful externally. Some spiritual masters become more and more successful in their cultural mission as they become neglectful internally. As a guru becomes weaker, he may attract more and more disciples who want an easy way and who want a spiritual master who does not pressure them to be disciplined and who assures them repeatedly that they will be saved. This attraction for popularity saves neither the spiritual master nor the disciples.

The spiritual master should maintain discipline and keep advancing further; otherwise, he will be degraded. Limited beings who act as spiritual masters must progress in austerity or face certain degradation.

Chapter 4

Envy and Popularity

Decrease of advancement due to envy

Another cause of degradation of the spiritual master is envy of God and envy of the predecessor authority who might be eternally greater than the spiritual master. Generally, the principle of acceptance of a spiritual master means that one acts as if the spiritual master is an eternal superior, even though in some cases, it is not so. For safety in dealing, the format is that one should assume the spiritual master as an eternal superior. However, if one is not completely purified, one might envy the spiritual master. One might envy his popularity and charisma which draws numerous human beings under his influence. One might become distracted in this way and neglect one's advancement and purification.

Many spiritual masters are not concerned about the purification of their disciples. They merely want a disciple they can use in a particular way. Once they find such a person they use him until his worth diminishes. In other words, they surround themselves with an army of assistants but have no genuine regard for an individual's spiritual welfare. This is satisfactory for most disciples who are not really interested in liberation, but who instead, want to fit into a niche in a spiritual society. In this way, there is mutual exploitation between a spiritual master and his disciples.

All this serves to kill any effort at purification and keeps the disciples in an impure stage which gives only imaginative freedom from material bondage.

Some spiritual masters stagnate because they envy material nature which has most of the souls under its direct control. Since these spiritual masters are frustrated in the efforts to liberate humanity on a mass scale, they develop an enmity towards material nature. Through such enmity they become stagnant in spiritual development even though their following may increase.

Popularity as cause of stagnation

The hunger for popularity, its acquirement and maintenance, effectively absorbs and diffuses the attention of most spiritual masters of repute. Popularity sabotages their spiritual life. It is one thing to be an unknown spiritual master in a village of India or a small corner of the world and it is an entirely different matter to be a well-known guru.

Fame is one of the most stubborn needs of the human being, not only in the spiritual field but also in every other aspect of human existence. Hardly a living entity wants to remain as an obscure, unknown, left-behind, disregarded side-feature of reality. Most of the teachers want rapid popularity. A few who do not care if they get it during this life time, work cautiously. Those who crave it during the current life have a tendency to take risks and do things haphazardly which usually results in the ruination of their missions. Fame is also related to spiritual elevation since by fame one is able to handle many of the responsibilities assigned by destiny. Without fame, it is impossible for certain spiritual masters to take care of their responsibilities towards the entities that they are required to liberate.

Fame is also a method of reaching the higher material planets. This is why the ancient rulers were willing to die in battle, feeling that if they died courageously rather than flee to safety, they would attain fame and heaven. A legend has it, that King Indrad remained in a heavenly kingdom for a long time through fame. When his stay in that paradise was exhausted, he reestablished his reputation and ascended to that heaven again without taking earthly rebirth.

In the *Mahabharata* account, the king fell from heaven when his earthly fame waned. Upon reaching the earth, he tried to locate any person or creature who remembered him, since he could return to heaven by the reminiscence. Indrad met a long-lived sage named Markan. The yogi did not recognize the king, whom he referred to an elder, which was an owl. The bird did not recognize the king, but referred him to its elder, which was a crane which lived at a reservoir named Indrad Lake. The crane did not remember him but sent him to its elder, an ancient tortoise. This reptile, Akupar, remembered the king. With tearful eyes and a fluttering heart, the tortoise recalled the religious ceremonies the king performed and the domestic animals he gave in charity. The tortoise said that the lake was created by the hoof prints of cattle donated by the king. As those words were spoken, a celestial conveyance appeared to take King Indrad back to paradise.

Is this just a legend? Is there some truth to this? As related, the king was dependent on earthly fame to remain in the heavenly kingdom. He was threatened for relocation to this earthly place if his fame were to wane. This gives us an important hint about many departed spiritual masters. These gurus need earthly fame for permanency on the celestial level. If the fame vanished, if no one practiced their principles on earth, they would again take an earthly body and develop a new preaching mission and again work to become famous and convince people to become morally reformed and to practice psychological disciplines, and then again return to the celestial places.

Chapter 5

Keeping in Touch
with Higher Authorities

Location

In spiritual life, there are essentially two types of gurus. One is the official type and the other is the unofficial type. Both types are necessary. In some cases the official and unofficial guru is the same person but invariably, a seeker requires more than one guru. A guru may only excel in a specific discipline. Therefore he cannot advise one in detail about other aspects. For information on these, one must go to a person with the required proficiency.

The official spiritual master might not have a technique one needs, or he might not have the time to train one personally even if he knows the required discipline. If one is serious, one may go to someone else, to an unofficial spiritual master, a person with whom one may have a casual relation but who is proficient.

Spiritual masters must continually take help from their spiritual master, from the Supreme Being and from other authorities who assist them.

Spiritual masters not only take help from their selected gurus, but from other spiritual masters as well but they are expert in hiding the sources of the inspiration. Some advanced souls who deliberately resist fame, and who do not become known to the general masses are more advanced than some who are famous. Some of these hidden masters are willing to help humanity indirectly by instructing the famous spiritual masters. They instruct these spiritual masters, give them techniques but all the while they remain hidden and act as if they know nothing. A spiritual master may also use advanced meditation techniques in secret when he is resting.

Some famous spiritual masters are unconsciously inspired by departed advanced souls who live in other dimensions. Some go into isolation or to a retreat and recharge themselves after becoming exhausted in dealing with degraded followers. Some take a vow of silence as a way of avoiding people for a week, month or year. In the meantime, they recharge themselves for another bout of degrading association.

Manifestation of mystic powers

The manifestation of mystic powers is part and parcel of being a spiritual master, for without mystic power, one cannot influence anyone. There is a game involved, however, in the expression of mystic power, since there are certain laws of nature that apply to the misuse of such energy. If a spiritual master misuses power, he faces reactions. In the yoga system of austerities, it is said that if one displays mystic power by performing miracles, one will more than likely become degraded. We see that in some cases the display of miracles produces positive results in terms of creating faith in the minds of followers.

Jesus Christ, for instance, displayed mystic power by instantly healing the sick, re-energizing dead bodies and producing food for large numbers of people who grew hungry after his lectures. Thus he caused people to have faith in God in so far as they felt that God has the power to alter material nature. Jesus had the courtesy to glorify God for the empowerment. He created theistic faith.

There was a successful yogi in India by the name of Yogesh. This writer met him on the astral level. When he was asked about mystic powers developed through yoga practice, he said this:

"My advice is that these psychic powers should not be used. When I used my recent material body, I displayed mystic power. My motive was to convince people to seriously undertake austerities. I was not trying to show off or anything like that. Since people were reluctant to take to the austerities, I did, for a little time, show mystic power as a way of encouragement. But, in some cases, it had a contrary effect. Some people did not take to my motivation but had their own idea that I should serve their needs. You see this in the life of Jesus Christ. He was just there to inform others of God, whom he regarded as his eternal father. He wanted to preach about the kingdom of God and the laws of God through which human beings may improve themselves, but people wanted him to raise dead relatives, heal the sick and produce bread and water.

"I had cases where people wanted me to save them from cancer or from a lawsuit or from some other mundane difficulty brought on by undesirable developments in their destinies. On occasion, circumstances demanded that I use my powers in that way. This, however, is a misuse of powers. I was circumstantially forced by followers. Gradually I learned not to display these powers. Once people become aware of your power, they insist on using it to overcome a difficulty. You will become like a banker or shopkeeper.

"If a man is hungry, he will go to a shop keeper for food. If someone is short on money, he will make friends with a banker to get a donation or loan. He may even rob the banker. In the same way, once people realize that there is mystic power in a certain man they will exploit him. If one does not cooperate, they will resent him. It is best not to display the powers. If someone develops such power in the course of transcendental practice, I advise him not to display it. He should continue the practice and pretend that he is just an ordinary person. Otherwise he will have to deal with a demanding public and more than likely, he will abuse himself.

"You have seen that many transcendentalists from India become famous all of a sudden. Then they get disciples all over the world, but many followers are contaminated. It is not easy to control one's relationships, once fame is achieved. If a spiritual master has a few disciples, he can control them, but as soon as he gets many, he loses control. The disciples begin to tap into his reserve energy. Therefore such power should not be displayed whimsically.

"If you study the life of Christ, you will see that in some cases, he was influenced by disciples or by the public. It is not that he used the mystic power of his own free selection on every occasion. Of course, in Christ's life, the use was positive as was proven in history by the extensive faith in God he transmitted for centuries. Still in some cases, he was influenced by others. Let us take an example of the story at sea. When he was in the Sea of Galilee, a storm arose. He slept, but his disciples were scared stiff even though most of them were fishermen and were familiar with sea storms. Still they woke him, crying, 'Master! Master! Get up! There is a storm. The boat sways this way and that way. We are afraid.' Actually this was a subtle request of theirs to get him to use mystic power because they knew he possessed it. In that circumstance he was pressured. Perhaps the boat was not destined to capsize. So perhaps there was really no necessity for use of the power.

"Again in the case of the centurion's servant, the centurion appealed to Jesus to heal his paralyzed servant. He said, 'I heard of your activities. I understand that you are a great mystic. Just say the word and my servant will be healed!' And Jesus, although reluctant, exercised his mystic abilities to heal the servant, just to satisfy the centurion's request.

"There are other reasons why one should not exhibit such power. If one miscalculates, one will suffer. Even in Christ's case, there is a story of a woman who drew power from Christ without asking him. He was in a crowd, so the Bible says, and then a woman touched him. She did not have permission. She was not one of his disciples, yet she drew power from him, so much power that Christ felt a power drain. He immediately said, 'Who touched me?' The woman admitted, and Christ forgave her. He did not chastise but he did not like it.

"Once a disciple wanted to be cured of a disease, I transmitted power. Then I found that I contracted the disease and had to lay down for a week or so to recover. This is called a power drain and it is due to a miscalculation. Even a person as great as Christ was affected noticeably when touched by the woman who knew he had power and who had every intention of getting a boost by being near him.

"In India we have the conception of Bhagavan or God. This usually refers to Lord Krishna or Lord Rama. They have power, but others do not have that much power. Our power is limited so if we miscalculate there will be disaster. If one passes urine in a jug, the water is ruined but if one passes urine in the sea, there is no visible effect. It is like that. Those of small power cannot safely absorb contamination. They should not leave themselves open to harm by displaying mystic power."

Bringing others under one's control

Some spiritual masters do not try to manifest miracles but specialize in the miracle of bringing others under their control. This is a particular mystic power of making someone do something regardless of his desire. In the modern history of Christianity, this power was greatly developed by the Reverend Norman Vincent Peale. He wrote a series of books on what he termed to be positive thinking. He spread the idea that a person could change unfavorable circumstances by thinking positively. He used prayers as a way of manifesting desires.

Some years ago a yogi explained a similar process to the writer. He said, "When I want to make a person do something, I approach the person in a charming way. I transmit my desire to him. Once the desire is transmitted, the person will speak of it as if it were his desire. I will say, 'Okay, that is a very good idea. See if you can manifest it.' In this way I used to influence many people to do what I wanted. They felt that it as a personal desire, while in fact, the thought originated from me. I never let them know I was the source of the idea. In using such powers, if I alerted the other person that he was being influenced, he usually resisted. I transmit the desire and remain quiet and just allow the person to act as if it is his desire. As soon as he mentions it, I respond by saying, "Yes, this is a very good idea. "

This is a form of psychology used by powerful personalities. This system of influencing others is even used by some religious leaders who condemn the use of mystic powers. For instance, there was a guru in India who was condemned for producing gold dust, gold ornaments and sacred ash, but some gurus who criticize him, use their charisma to amass huge followings and use disciples to fulfill desires for worldwide fame. All the while their disciples are generally naive as to how they are being influenced by the critical teacher.

The influence of people, however, is part and parcel of existence and it cannot be stopped. What we are concerned with in the spiritual field is the abuse of the power by taking persons away from their cultural destiny, twisting their lives, giving them false promises and keeping them under one's influence without actually helping them on the spiritual path. People will be influenced no matter what, because that is the way of the world but the influence should be for the person's benefit.

A spiritual master who passes off every one of his desires as God's desire and who convinces his followers of this, misuses them because so much of a spiritual master's life is personal, having little to do with God in the strictest sense. Therefore a spiritual master should be honest enough to let disciples know the contrast between his personal desires and God's.

A spiritual master should also be concerned enough about a disciple that he may advise the disciple not to assist him in certain areas of his mission since such assistance may be harmful to the follower.

There are times when a disciple should cultivate himself rather than assist the authority. If the spiritual master influences the disciple at these times and causes the disciple to neglect personal disciplines, a fault will be incurred and eventually the relationship will deteriorate.

Some spiritual masters misuse disciples by creating a martial spirit, where the disciples become fanatical to fulfill the plans of the guru. Under the teacher's influence, the disciple does many vicious acts to get money or to gain popularity for the teacher. In the end, however, the disciple and spiritual master are imperiled. Thus the mystic power for influencing others, is the most dangerous mystic power for the transcendentalist.

Strength of a spiritual master

The real strength of a spiritual master is his resistance to vice. This means resistance to subtle and gross vice. His power actually comes from such resistance but he may depart from the moral way and take to immoral activities if he is desperate for popularity. To develop wholesome mystic power, to be a saint, one has to cease all immorality. A pious entity is not supposed to act criminally but due to the nature of the senses, he might deviate. After accumulating some power, he may commit criminal acts through the force of uncontrollable desires.

The resistance to vice is used by some to develop power and then due to bad motivation they return to criminal ways. One should maintain the resistance to vices even if one stops the austerities. The best course is to continue the penance to a degree and to maintain the moral ways but sometimes we relax to enjoy hard-earned austerities and thus our cultural life deteriorates.

Disciples also have a tendency to encourage the spiritual master in flattery. They over-praise his mission and tell how great he is and what great things he did or will do. In most cases, the spiritual master is so limited that he cannot save his most confidential disciples and still they flatter him.

Practically, each spiritual master thinks, "I will convert the world. I will get the country under control. I will save humanity. I have the perfect program."

The success of a spiritual master

The success of a spiritual master depends on two factors, namely, worthy disciples and sincere relationship with the predecessor. The sincere relation with the predecessor spiritual master is the most important aspect. The spiritual master does continue the mission of his spiritual master like a new runner in a tag team. Each runner takes a pole from the predecessor and continues the race. If a runner goes astray, however, he is not appreciated. He has to stay on the main track and deliver the pole to the next starter.

Some Tibetans have a system of recalling their spiritual master to his mission as soon as he takes rebirth. They try to identify the new parents of their departed teacher. As soon as a body is formed for him, they go and induce the parents to release him for reorientation and training. During the training, they test to see if they identified the correct personality.

The idea is that a transcendentalist may return to the material world to continue austerities and teaching services. It is an on-going system. Thus the spiritual master is reliant on worthy disciples who are supposed to be souls who were performing austerities and preaching in their previous lives and who have again come out in material bodies to complete their spiritual responsibilities. If a spiritual master cannot find worthy disciples, his alternative is to write books so that in the future, worthy people may find his teachings and utilize them.

The connection between the spiritual master and his departed teacher is a psychic one. It works through telepathic communication and mystic visionary experiences. These, however, can be misinterpreted if one has faulty mystic perception. Some spiritual masters try to leave detailed instructions in writing and still in such cases, when unusual incidences arise, the disciples try to contact them on the psychic plane to get opinions and recommendations.

The lineage

The legend of Vishwa is interesting. He wanted to be recognized as a saint, but he was denied. He had to discipline himself until his aggressive attitude was reformed, after which his nature changed and he was accepted. It was altered to such a degree that even though he knew what to do to discipline criminals and enemies of the state, he tolerated provocation. Instead he appealed to King Dasharath to allow Prince Rama to challenge the aggressors. At the time, Rama supposedly did not know the sounds used to invoke the required weapons. Vishwa taught Rama the pronunciations which Rama used to kill the demoness Tatika and her son Subahu as well as others who threatened saintly ascetics.

The lineage is a system of training given in disciplic succession from an established authority. When one enters the succession, one must comply with the current authority. If one cannot, one is not accepted. The current authority may be upright or he may be deviant to a degree but if one wants to be recognized as a formal disciple, one has to do as he says. There are flaws in the disciplic succession and these were indicated in the Bhagavad Gītā, where Krishna spoke of the necessity of establishing the succession again. Nevertheless, if one wants to enter the succession, one has to accept the current authority, regardless of the real or imagined deviations.

Once one accepts the leader and renders service, one is considered to be part of the succession. One is then authorized to act as part of the established system. This is how it works. The system can be abused by the current leader or by a follower. That possibility of abuse is always a factor because of faulty human nature.

As far as the empowered spiritual masters are concerned, some of them enter the succession but some do not. For instance, Buddha is definitely a divine being but he abandoned more than one succession. In fact, he worked in defiance to the established teachers to establish his own view.

Jesus Christ is also undoubtedly a divine person. He did not accept a Vedic lineage; at least the Bible gives no record of such acceptance. He accepted a Jewish lineage from Abraham and Moses through John the Baptist.

In all cases of acceptance, whether it is a Vedic line or some other system like Judaism or whether the authority simply accepts no system and begins a new line starting with himself like Buddha, there is the difficult task of adjusting the succession. Some spiritual masters say that there should be no adjustment but in fact, even these gurus do some adjusting according to time and place. Particularly in modern times, the idea of no adjustment of the succession is a very impractical one. Without adjustment, no ancient succession can work in the modern setting. Modern people make cultural and technological leaps and bounds which are incompatible to ancient cultures.

The whole idea behind "incarnations of Godhead" is adjustment of something that is not working in a religious system. The divine people come or they send an agent who can look at the situation and implement reforms. If he comes and makes the adjustment by discretion and it gives inadequate results they again send another agent. He tries and if that does not work, they send yet another agent who again tries.

Followers of each agent like to believe that whatever their authority establishes will succeed but it is not that simple because in modern times, everything is culturally mixed-up and trends disrupt established traditions. In the modern era, religions have to adjust continuously or they are rejected, left on the side as a botheration to human progress. This is why we see so many new religions and religious leaders springing up on the globe.

Religious fanatics like to feel that some ancient systems will work, but they forget that even such a system was established on the basis of a particular culture. In that sense, it is adjustable. If the cultural setting changes, the system as it is, in its ideal form, must be adjusted at least until we can get human beings back to the original tradition or cultural function. Until then everything is fantasy unless we adapt the system. But changing the system is a very delicate art that should only be done by an empowered agent who has divine authority to make such vital adjustment. If it is done by anyone else, it will create havoc and merely complicate the issue.

The empowered spiritual master or his agent can miscalculate. But we as human beings try to close our eyes and our minds to this possibility. If we think that he is perfect then it is easy to submit to him and do as he says. Therefore to help to submit, we like to believe that he does not make mistakes or that if he makes one, there is some great plan behind it. In this way we encourage the spiritual master in arrogance and an overgrown sense of confidence. We accelerate the ruination of his mission.

Let us take the example of a master who comes from India. His overall performance depends on his childhood upbringing, schooling, education, austerities from the past and present lives, and the empowerment he is endowed with. Still he may make mistakes. He was in India. He tried there. He was not successful. And yet, we take pride in thinking that his failure there was due to every other reason but his mistakes.

Someone may conclude that he was a failure in India, because the Indians took him for granted since there are so many yogis, swamis and transcendentalists on every street corner in every village of India.

He migrated to a developed country and became successful to a degree. But does he really understand Western culture? If our chosen guru is so all-knowing, so perceptive, why is it that he has to rely on Western disciples who know the Western culture thoroughly? Obviously, the guru is limited. He takes help because he has to, because he cannot see all the angles. He has to rely on others who are equipped with the knowledge, ability and cultural habits that are needed for the fulfillment of his mission.

Again, even after he relies on disciples, he may still make mistakes because they may give him only a partial view according to their limited experience. Therefore the idea that the guru is perfect in all circumstances is a false one. We support such an idea to ease ourselves and to boost our sense of security, but it hurts the spiritual master and his mission since the more he feels that he is perfect, the more he feels that his decisions and strategies are God-sent, the more he plans in a careless way.

Arrogance is part of leadership. Without arrogance one cannot tell others what to do. One would not dare. But when arrogance is over-extended, it produces a false sense of confidence; it produces a system of belief that allows the spiritual master to miscalculate.

In some cases, the spiritual master realizes his limitations and finds a disciple who can fulfill his mission. For instance, Jesus Christ had some difficulty getting the people of his time to accept his religious doctrine. Thus Jesus was crucified because common Jews and leading Jews alike, considered him to be an upstart, a pretender, a man wanting to be a god, a pauper pretending that he was a king. Later on, even after he departed the material body, Jesus converted the military commander, Saul, who later became known as Saint Paul, who molded Christianity into its present form.

Paul got rid of the more transcendental aspects of Christianity and made it more mundane but his adjustment was practical. Christianity succeeded even though it lost most of the transcendental aspects which Jesus imparted into it. By stripping away much of the transcendence and by giving facility for Roman culture, Paul gave Christianity a broader appeal and the religion spread to Gentile countries, the foreign lands. Later on many evangelists made further adjustments to keep Christianity as a major religion.

Being in the lineage automatically means functioning under certain restrictions but usually the empowered spiritual master or his agent makes adjustments to suit their time. These adjustments which are departures in one way or another, do become a new standard, at least until another agent appears and adjusts what was recently established.

Chapter 6

Limitations of the Guru

Human nature

Human nature is a limitation of a guru. It is also an asset of the guru, for by understanding the human psyche, he can better create practical disciplines. However, the same human nature may cause the guru to adjust too far away from the standard.

Human nature in the guru makes the guru establish lower standards while stating that these are sufficient for perfection. After establishing this, he attracts followers who feel comfortable following his method. But the disciplines may not be sufficient for salvation and the followers may become stagnant after mastering the recommended process to a satisfactory degree. Human nature is so designed that we do not feel comfortable unless we have a particular set of indulgences and a particular set of restrictions. Once we are oriented to these, we relax and stagnate.

Wealth addiction

Wealth addiction is another quality in question. Many gurus begin as paupers, as poor, unknown men with lofty ideas. Then, all of a sudden, popularity strikes, then money comes, then comfortable accommodations, then honor from every quarter and then all of a sudden the guru feels flattered since, in his view, providence facilitated him. At that point he enjoys ever-increasing finances. His sense of power grows beyond bounds. The initial poverty-stricken condition of the guru does not necessarily reveal his simplicity of mind. In fact, he might not be a simple person. He might be elaborate and aristocratic. When popularity and wealth overtake him, his real nature stands out as he becomes flushed in flattery, accommodations and fame.

When asked about the wealth that surrounds them and the various materialistic aspects of their missions, most gurus rush for excuses to stay clear of criticism. Eventually they learn to give standard answers. Some say it is God-given. Some say that it is the offerings of their disciples. Others say that they are immune just like the lotus leaf which floats on water but never absorbs it.

One spiritual master I knew began his community in total poverty. In fact, initially, he and a few followers were in abject poverty and had little to eat. We heard him say once that they ate partially rotten potatoes. Sometimes they almost starved. In any case, he stayed on and gradually more and more people came and then money came, popularity came. The neighbors began to fear the expansion. Gradually he constructed buildings. Then one year, all of a sudden he had so much money that he did not know what to do with it. He was so happy that he grinned from ear to ear.

He was asked about the money since people felt he said one thing about austerity but displayed indulgence. He explained that God gave the money because he was mature enough in spiritual detachment not to be carried away by it. Later, however, this explanation came to question because it was revealed that he was power-hungry and was involved in criminal activities. His greed for money only increased; it never diminished.

If, as he said, God gave him that wealth, then God only gave it for his ruination to expose him as being immature in spiritual leadership. But if God did not give the money to him, then on what basis did he attract it? Did destiny offer it to him in trickery? Why did he not recognize this? Was it offered to him because he had impure desires? Why did he not recognize this and become purified since he was following what he considered to be a bona fide process? Why was he, an agent for the divine, bound hand and foot by material wealth and carried away until he was totally corrupted?

Fame addiction

Fame addiction is another problem for the gurus. In the initial stage when a guru is unknown, he does not have to worry about achieving it. In the beginning, he is usually satisfied because he gets fulfillment from performing austerities. He thinks deeply in isolation, being free from demanding relationships. Later on, when the fame comes, it lifts him up and carries him from one great city to another.

Some gurus run away from fame when it seeks them. Some stand and deal with it, either losing or winning the battle for not being controlled by it. Some who have dormant desires for lordship, try to control fame but they become a slave to it. Eventually they begin to act as impediments to the divine vision.

Instead of assisting the followers, a guru may hamper them by presenting himself openly or covertly as God. In this way he obstructs the view of God and pretends that he has universal power.

The spiritual master's obligations to disciples

Generally, we feel that there is a one-way obligation, that of the disciple to the spiritual master. Actually the obligation is two-way, that of the spiritual master to disciple and the disciple to the authority in turn. In some instances, it gets competitive where the disciple gets so far ahead of the spiritual master that the authority feels pressured to reciprocate with his dependent disciple. In some instances, the spiritual master begins a relationship with a false promise. When he does this, he is forced to pay the disciple in a materialistic way on demand.

For success in preaching missions and to ward off competition, a spiritual master may assure the public, "Follow me. Follow my process. In a short time, salvation will be yours. I offer the purest, speediest form of salvation. Other teachers make false promises. Try my method. It is easy and enjoyable with very little austerity. It gives immediate happiness."

However, if people join him, serve and become stagnant, they begin to wonder if they were cheated. Some go away and criticize him. Some join other groups. Some remain and pressure him to yield a result. The award of official positions is a common method of payback to loyal disciples. The spiritual master may say, "I appoint you as the president. Teach authoritatively." Or he might reward by saying, "I declare to all that you are advanced. They will respect you just as they do me." In these ways and in others, a spiritual master cheats a disciple by not giving what the follower really desires, which is spiritual advancement.

On the other hand, some disciples who acquire positions, are people who were themselves ill-motivated. They wanted a comfortable, secure post in a religious organization. They did not want on-going spiritual progress which requires steady, consistent day to day effort. When the position was offered they accepted and became stagnant.

A famous spiritual master is more likely to abuse himself and his organization in the way of awarding positions to disciples by giving the false impression to one and all that these are spiritual awards. Those spiritual masters who resist fame are less likely to do so. They may train disciples more carefully and spend more time making sure that the followers develop spiritually.

Another handy method used by spiritual masters is the one of entertaining the disciples with raspy, critical philosophical discourses which in fact does nothing for the advancement of disciples. But this does help the disciples to feel better about themselves in reference to others.

In India, one tradition is that a spiritual master sends disciples out each day to collect alms. Originally, this was done without intimidating the public. Nowadays, however, the public is unwilling to give alms to the real and false holy men. Thus disciples are forced, more or less, to intimidate people in order to get sufficient donations. The disciples go out and collect money in one way or another, under one name or another. In doing this, they are harassed by the public. Since they have to pinch people, wring necks, take verbal abuses and intimidation and in some cases practically prostitute themselves and sacrifice their principles to get sufficient funds or goods to complete the services specified by the guru, they usually go back daily, weekly or monthly to the guru with the specific money and goods along with the resentments and frustrations acquired.

First of all the guru usually has a front man, a secretary or agent who first greets these begging, collecting disciples of his. Their collections are listed. This listing is required by law in some counties where the government closely scrutinizes the religious groups to be sure that they are not abusing privileges as registered non-profit societies. After the listing is made, it is presented to the spiritual master. Depending on his monetary needs, he assesses the list in one way or another.

Usually he greets the collecting disciples in a cordial way. He encourages them to go out and collect again. He congratulates them in general and specifically mentions those who brought in large sums of money or commodities. He praises those who converted the greatest number of new followers on that particular day, week, or month. After this, there is more pep talk. Then a discussion ensues. The disciples usually ask questions having to do with encounters with the public whereby someone refused to give willingly, refused to buy holy books or goods, or verbally criticized them outright. The spiritual master begins his reply. In part, he deals with the statements of opponents by telling the disciples how to give counteracting views. He may give examples of how they should have responded. In part, the guru begins to deride the opponents in no uncertain terms.

This ridicule is greatly loved by some disciples and it is so sweet to their ears and minds that they immediately forget the hardship and intimidation and become eager to face the challenges of another collection trip. However, in some of this ridicule of the opponents, the spiritual master neglects his disciples in the sense that he does not further their enthusiasm to make spiritual progress. He ruthlessly conveys the impression that the collection effort is spiritual progress.

Spiritual masters who are less mean and more compassionate, who are concerned about spiritual advancement, give each of the followers a constructive, tailored piece of advice that might include criticism of the same disciple's tactics along with a recommended discipline which the person should assume for self-reform.

Grabbing the disciples of others

A favorite method of spiritual masters is to grab the disciples of other gurus. This frequently causes offenses that lead to the downfall of a grabbing guru, or to the ruination of his mission. Few spiritual masters are not eager to grab but even these find that they must deal with the followers of others. They too are required by circumstance to develop a general policy in regard to the spiritual seekers who come from another spiritual society. In grabbing the disciples of others, some spiritual masters increase their name and fame and advertise what they term as their potency. However the disciple-grabbing technique causes tangles amongst spiritual masters, with some invariably getting hurt in the process. Some spiritual masters feel that they have broad authority to convert the world, either during their lifetime or from the world hereafter. Such leaders inspire disciples to convert one and all but invariably mistakes are made, offenses are committed and ruination follows.

It is a rare spiritual master who does not have such a grabbing attitude, who has a general policy of non-interference, and who assists those from other groups without trying to dominate, thus allowing them to gradually hear, associate and decide for themselves what to do.

The ego problem

Spiritual masters do have an ego problem. Depending on the level of advancement, they either dispose of it or nurture it. Some do not perceive an ego problem but these usually think that everyone has an ego except themselves. Since they feel that they are the most surrendered persons, they are not objective to arrogance.

Allowing others to lead is one way to ease the ego problem, but if the guru allows others to lead as extensions of his own ego, then there is no ease for him. Others may lead, but in doing so, the spiritual master would have to act as an ordinary follower for the time being to get rid of his ego.

Those who have an overgrown ego attract followers who flatter them, recommend them, and fully support their grand delusions, but these spiritual masters eventually come to ruination.

Once a spiritual master becomes hung up or attached to himself as a leading authority, his ruination is certain either in this world or the next. It is inevitable since sooner or later he will lose the following when he departs the body and must again adjust himself to being an unknown. The mere idea that he was unknown in his earlier life and that no one took him seriously, indicates that this may be repeated. And once he leaves the world, he might all of a sudden, find himself in a higher world with higher personalities under whose gaze he might feel insignificant. To be a spiritual master and to entirely or conveniently forget that one is subordinate to higher authorities, is a great blunder.

Limiting the realizations of disciples

If a spiritual master is limited in realization, he will automatically limit the understanding of disciples and only the very perceptive ones will be able to get beyond him. By human nature a spiritual master is very suspicious of anyone who is more intelligent than himself, especially if that person happens to be his disciple. Thus when there is any question that challenges his actions or any questions that might reveal his limited understanding, he will effectively brush the question aside, cover it, shift to another topic or use some other survival tactic to maintain his status.

Those disciples who are lazy, who want to relax and coast along, will appreciate a stagnant process which does not evolve further nor requires the followers to keep upgrading their self-reform

To be honest with himself, a disciple has to know what he requires from a particular spiritual master. He should be willing to pay the price dictated by the guru. He must also have enough sense to go to others for badly needed techniques that he cannot get from an authority who may be conversant with one aspect of spiritual life and be totally ignorant of others.

Chapter 7

Misuse of Mystic Power

Acquirement and Misuse of Mystic Power

As we stated before, the spiritual master must have mystic power. Those who serve as spiritual teachers and who profess that they have no mystic power or those who deride others who display energy, are simply using a ploy to accredit themselves with saintliness.

The mystic power must be there in a spiritual master. Its use and abuse is in question. By his motive, he uses the power in one way or another, but it will be used by him. Any leader in the religious or political field is using mystic power. It is mandatory and so much of a spiritual master's control over followers is political or social control also. Most of the spiritual masters are not satisfied simply to give instructions about religion. They extend their rule into social portions of the lives of the disciples. Thus, many temples and hermitages have adjoining dormitories to house disciples.

In India, usually the ashrams are for male students of the spiritual master. These are mostly single men. When the master comes from India to the Western countries, he usually extends shelter to married couples and single women as well. Thus his political and social interest in the lives of disciples is revealed. In turn, critics cry, "Cult! Cult! This man runs a cult whereby he dominates every aspect of the lives of disciples. "

The misuse of mystic power by the spiritual masters is done on the basis of four factors, namely:

- *the connection of the spiritual master with his predecessor*
- *his bad motivation*
- *his susceptibility to the influence of followers*
- *absorption of envy from others*

The connection of the spiritual master with his predecessor

The spiritual master acquires spiritual power or charisma through a higher authority. The acquirement implies that the spiritual master must fulfill some desires of the predecessor. If he tricks the predecessor and does not fulfill the mission placed upon him as an obligation, he loses grace and is vacated of controlling abilities. Gradually he misuses the power more and more, becomes ugly in the eyes of followers and falls in the opinion of the public.

When the power is used to attract and control others, it is called charismatic power and when it is used to heal the sick, raise the dead and to reverse apparent laws of nature, it is called miracles or mystic power.

In these situations, it is the same mystic power, even though the use varies. Some spiritual masters manage to trick disciples into thinking that the means to reversing the laws of nature is mystic power and the means to attract believers is devotion. But in all cases it is mystic power. In fact, attracting believers and converts, can also be done with a bad motivation to lord it over the human race unnecessarily. Gurus, who indulge in this, reach certain ruination when their preaching mission suddenly expands and then it shrinks and shrinks and shrinks inexplicably.

Using the elements of gross potencies of nature to create miracles is one of the forms of misuse of the power. Misusing human beings is a greater offense against nature particularly if it involves fooling people, while convincing them that one acts on behalf of God.

Another more subtle offense in the relationship between the spiritual master and his predecessor is the predecessor's bad motivations which filtered into the nature of the present spiritual master. Generally, one believes that the spiritual master is perfect. Therefore, if he is not absolutely perfect and if he is indeed partially corrupt, there is every chance that his corrupt nature will infect disciples. Thus, whenever the power passes, corruption will also. This will complicate matters, since even a little impurity of his predecessor will create in the present spiritual master, a complicated set of bad motivations which will result in the misuse of mystic powers.

Since mystic power cannot be avoided, spiritual masters should study and practice the laws of its good usage. When a spiritual master becomes famous, he usually feels that providence blessed him. He begins to do any and everything. He steps on the laws of morality and ruins himself. This is historic. It repeats itself in the life of one spiritual master after another. Human nature is there even in a spiritual master and so errors are inevitable.

It may be surprising that some devotional spiritual masters, who profess to follow moral principles, do encourage their disciples to perform dishonest or criminal activities for the collection of funds and for increasing the number of disciples. This happens in the name of God.

One spiritual master who wanted to have huge temples all over the world, used to encourage followers to raise large sums of money by any means. He used to tell the public that the money came in from the sale of his books. But actually, his books were not selling as he said. They were being distributed but the sales were not bringing in as much money as he said. Much of the money was acquired by badgering people in public places, selling narcotics and other illicit activities and practices. In any case, he drove his leading disciples in this way. He falsely stated that all funds were acquired through donations and the sale of his books. In this enthusiasm, he did not closely check to see how the money was being raised under pressure from his demands, nor did he observe how senior disciples got money in illegal ways, as long as they could satisfy his request for funds. Eventually his society was ruined.

This is a clear exhibition of a careless greed for success in a spiritual master. He used charismatic power to influence the disciples to do any and everything to meet his financial goals. This is an exhibition of corrupted mystic power.

A spiritual master who is in such a hurry for fame that he fails to cultivate mystic perception, a spiritual master who is convinced that he must become famous in the lifetime of his body, and who cannot wait for gradual results, will invariably deviate from the path of morality and in doing so, he declares war on human society. Even if he does this in the name of God, the spiritual master will have to battle against gross nature and supernatural nature. He may lose the battle, as God may not come to his aid. His mission will see certain shrinkage and failure.

The spiritual master's bad motivation

Bad motivation in a living being is discovered by two methods:

- **self discovery through introspection**
- **public discovery by circumstantial pressure**

While one is merely a disciple of a spiritual master trying to improve in spiritual life, there is a chance for introspection, but as soon as one becomes a spiritual master, one is concerned with the development of others and of necessity, one neglects self-reform.

Unfortunately, by human nature, a spiritual master who is discovered to be faulty may cover up his mistakes in an attempt to restore the public image. Therefore, instead of humbly admitting the defect, he will assert himself with greater force and cover up until he appears to be the ugliest human being on the surface of the globe.

The least painful way of correcting bad motivation or a persistent fault in one's nature, is to do some serious introspection. Material nature helps us by revealing faults at every step. If we are attentive to actions and consequences, we will see the miscalculations and will not have to be shown by others. Then we can take the task to correct ourselves by deliberate adjustment within the psyche. This means that we have to enact in our lives, some moral principles and continually improve these until our sense of conscience is acutely sharpened. Once this is done it will be near impossible to do anything exploitive or criminal.

If after becoming a spiritual master, one does not introspect or spend time with one's self in deep consideration of further development, one's remaining faults will be shown by material nature through circumstantial pressure. Even though as a spiritual master, a man may give up his bid for perfection and start believing that he is in perfection, material nature will not be convinced even though his followers may be. Nature will attack him at every step to expose the dishonesty.

The supernatural people know of a spiritual master's defects. They too, will set up conditions to expose him. The spiritual master, being trigger-happy over success and being flattered by disciples, will be unaware of the supernatural people and their operations and will fall into one of their traps. All the while, he might believe that he has immunity from being disgraced and that he is protected by the divine. In the end, even some of his dear most followers will denounce him.

The supernatural people do, however, give a spiritual master a chance to adjust. They do so by pushing him into minor hassles. If he continues in an immoral way, they increase the complexity until the spiritual master enters a valley of sorrow.

Becoming a spiritual master is a dangerous step for any aspiring transcendentalist. However, it cannot be avoided, but it should be tempered by having a small number of disciples and by controlling those disciples strictly in terms of creating a relationship which is tightly regulated on the basis of spiritual disciplines and moral upliftment. A spiritual master should not use disciples to fulfill personal ambitions for to do so is dangerous. There is a thin line between the mission of God and the personal desires of the guru. If he confuses this, he is implicated for misusing disciples.

Some spiritual masters feel that they are totally surrendered to their departed guru or to God or both agencies simultaneously. They feel that they have no personal desire. But this is a fallacy because no one can be that surrendered to anyone at any time. The mere idea that we have individual natures means that we must have some personal desire and motivation, either for good or for bad. Therefore the spiritual master is dishonest if he pretends that he has no personal self or that he has no personal desire. He must have these since the individual nature of the living being is asserted by Krishna in the Bhagavad Gītā.

> There was never a time when I did not exist, nor you nor these rulers of the people. Nor will we cease to exist from now onwards. (2.12)

Thus the spiritual master should honestly try to fulfill personal desires and work conjointly with disciples to fulfill God's or the predecessor's plans. Many spiritual masters demand that their disciples tend to them in a personal way as a fee for giving initiation or position or some other status. This is against the spiritual law. Those who make such demands are eventually ruined.

There are numerous cases of spiritual masters who used disciples to fulfill personal desires as a sort of pay off to the guru. In the *Mahabharata* legend, there is the case of Drona, who after teaching the Kuru princes in military schools, insisted at their graduation that they pay him by seizing King Drupad and his kingdom. This they did. Later, Drona was killed in an inglorious way by Drupad's son, Indrad. In some cases, however, the result does not manifest as ruination. It all depends on whether it is a pious or impious act. However, we still advise spiritual masters to refrain from using disciples in that way.

Essentially, a disciple is entrusted to the spiritual master for the sake of spiritual advancement in assisting in the mission of God and not so much for helping the spiritual master with visions of grand delusions and his personal gripes against destiny and society.

The spiritual master's susceptibility to the influence of others

Usually a spiritual master has high hopes for success when he begins a preaching mission. At the initial point he has concentrated power that has not been diluted by a mix of energy from disciples. With this concentrated power and with ideas for saving a sector of humanity, a spiritual master starts out to win or lose according to the opportunities afforded to him by providence.

Without realizing that this initial point is the high point in their development, most spiritual masters proceed looking for another high point which to their mind will be the point of their greatest popularity. In most cases, however, the spiritual master becomes popular at his weakest point, since material nature and destiny has what is called a time lag in the manifestation of matching energies.

However, the spiritual master starts out and gradually he takes more and more disciples which means more and psychic pollution. He may be compared to a woman who frequently becomes pregnant and is bothered with the sum-total mischievous nature of the children she bears.

Some spiritual masters who find that they are being dragged down by disciples, quickly shut down their missions, pull down the missionary placards and disappear. Some return to India and hide in some insignificant village and others go elsewhere, being scared stiff of reactions coming as a result of mixing with disciples whom they are unable to control.

Other spiritual masters who are more courageous and who are more possessed of a strong sense of mission, do not relent. When they fail, their bodies and minds fall sick. They are dragged through scandals or through legal courts to answer the charges about their disciples' misconduct. Then, when they realize that there is a danger, they shift the trouble to their power-hungry followers who want positions. At that time, the spiritual master may call one leading disciple and say, "I am old now. It is time for me to retire. You take charge. Manage this nicely. Everyone will be looking to you as the new leader under my authority."

In that polite way, the spiritual master moves away from social complexities and leaves his naive senior disciples in the mess. When a spiritual master begins missionary activities, he usually only sees the bright light. He does not see the liabilities or the social opposition he will reach by the complexities of destiny that will be thrown in his path. Thus he miscalculates. Therefore part of the faults and reactions that are coming to his disciples, come to him in part and burden him down. He may feel that God will remove these since he feels that he is one hundred percent for God, but invariably he himself has to carry the burden. If he is not very powerful, he is overwhelmed by it.

The absorption of envy of others

Spiritual masters usually don't calculate that they will receive tons of envy and bad energy from others. When the negative energy comes they usually sulk, saying, "This is unfair. They do not appreciate my mission. I am working for God. Why are they attacking me? They are demons. We are good people. We will prevail."

Some spiritual masters calculate the envy and resentment but dismiss it as irrelevant, feeling that God will nullify it since they work for God. In the meantime, public resentment builds up to an explosive level. If we study the life of Jesus, we will see that even though he was empowered for the occasion and even though he did not encourage immorality, still he had to face resentment. At one time, he almost turned him away from God when he was depressed in the Garden of Gethsemane. In the end, Christ decided to face it rather than to run away. He absorbed it efficiently during the crucifixion. The resentment of human beings against any sort of good or bad change is a fact and justifiably or unjustifiably spiritual masters are victimized by it.

Besides human society, there is material nature which does not easily release the disciples of a spiritual master. The spiritual master must fight material nature to get disciples released, step by step. Anytime he relaxes, material nature recaptures the disciples. Usually, a spiritual master's promise about freeing disciples from material bondage is mostly empty words, because material nature is unwilling to free any conditioned entity. What occurs is that the disciples remain partly bound and partly free and gradually if the spiritual master is not careful, material nature claims his mission and makes it into a total failure.

The idea of some spiritual masters that God will absorb the resentment is a foolish notion of theirs, but they do sincerely think in this way. According to the history of Jesus Christ, he himself took up the resentment for the work he did in reforming so many human beings. And even today, resentment is channeled to him for the religion he created, even though he is not physically present. Therefore a spiritual master has to take up the resentment and the glory involved and not just believe that he will get the glory and transfer the liabilities to God.

Incidentally, Jesus did sanction an act of theft when his disciples appropriated corn on the Sabbath. Generally, however, he did not allow them to circumvent law and order. When Peter sliced off the ear of a Roman soldier who was sent to arrest Christ, Jesus chastised Peter and miraculously restored the soldier's ear.

Chapter 8

Use of Mystic Power

Historic control of the world

Some spiritual masters refrain from using mystic power to control material nature and to perform miracles but instead they instinctively focus on accelerating the history of the world. Their intention is to leave their mark on human civilization. For that matter, being a spiritual master means leaving an impact on the world; for a spiritual master can only show his effectiveness by pushing human civilization in a desired direction.

Jesus Christ, for instance, made his impact first on Western society and practically moved the entire Roman civilization in the direction desired. Later, his followers swerved a large sector of humanity. Jesus' influence was felt in all areas: political, artistic, financial and in practically every aspect of human sociology. His influence continues to this day. Thus every spiritual master is in a hustle to leave a mark on the world before his body departs. A person like Jesus Christ, however, works in such a way that he does not care if he makes an impact in his own lifetime, but he carefully sets his energy in such a way that his impact prevails even after he departs, while other spiritual masters are eager to see full success during their lifespan.

In the strict sense, all spiritual masters are carried away by manifest destiny which involves being caught up in the social history of the world and mixing spiritual austerities with human needs. Such a mixing process dilutes everything and waters down the potency to such an extent that none of the followers are liberated by the impotent process given, even though the followers do believe with all sincerity and conviction that they will be released at the time of death. In that sense, most of these religious systems are farces. The spiritual masters are dishonest since they cannot release any follower by the watered-down austerities and religions they present.

Since most followers have no mystic vision, and since they berate the accomplishment of it and distrust it, they cannot see into the hereafter. They cannot check to see if the spiritual master is being dishonest. In other words, there is no way for them to verify whether salvation was possible for any follower who passed on before them. There is nothing stronger in human psychology than conviction. Whether a conviction is true or false, proven or unproven, it may hold the attention of a human being even if it leads nowhere and is merely a figment of imagination. Such is the limitation of human nature.

Generally, when the spiritual leader passes away, the followers advocate that he is liberated. They carefully package his religious views in a wrapping of security. In this way, they make certain that his religious doctrine becomes standardized. In the meantime, the spiritual master maneuvers from the world hereafter. He operates from the dream world, the astral world. From there he enthuses followers to preach his doctrine, to remember him and to convert others. The story of Jesus Christ which is presented in the New Testament shows this clearly. After Christ passed away, many fantastic stories spread about him, especially about his glaring appearance to some important disciples. People were astonished to hear these tales. Only the chief disciples checked to see if the stories were true, but people accepted the legends at face value because of the strength of the conviction with which they were told.

The people were socially suppressed by the Romans. They clung to the hope given by Jesus Christ. Gradually, the Romans realized that the man they crucified was still giving them trouble. His following increased even after his death was pronounced. His followers said that Christ survived death, and that he appeared visually even after his body was laid in a tomb. Since the following was growing, the Romans, being ever alert to protect their government in the countries they occupied, felt the necessity to suppress it, to snuff out the risk of rebellion. A Roman officer named Saul was appointed to wipe out the followers of Jesus Christ. His orders were clear; to simply kill or persecute the followers. So Saul took up these orders and began a systematic persecution of the early Christians.

It is said that in the hereafter, Christ took affront to these attacks. He attacked Saul by striking him down on a road with a blinding light.

Exactly how Jesus Christ did this is not clearly explained to this day. No one has figured out exactly what happened but Saul was blinded by light. He was circumstantially forced to accept the divinity of Jesus Christ. He submitted himself to one of Jesus' followers and became a staunch adherent, assuming the name of Paul. As Paul, he spread Christianity systematically. He used administrative skill to establish the religion, a task that Jesus failed to achieve prior to the crucifixion.

One may surmise that Saul was simply struck by a bolt of lightning, but if that was all there was to it, why did he hear a voice asking him to account for the persecution of Christ's followers? Why did Saul surrender to Christ's mission thereafter and dedicate himself fully to it?

It must be that these empowered spiritual masters do not rest after departing their material bodies, but rather they work from the hereafter to expand their religion in one way or another. They use as much mystic power as they can wield from the spirit world.

There are many convincing stories from every type of religion in the world, of persons who met a religious leader in a dream or vision and became converted to the master's mission in such a way and with such conviction that the person exhibited a radical change in lifestyle and shed his usual purposes to take up the mission of the said departed teacher.

The evidence is there for all to see: These departed spiritual masters work from the dream world and influence people on this side of existence.

The idea that they work from a higher level is not a false one, but it does not have much bearing because the higher level makes contact with this world through the dream world. Regardless of the level attained by the spiritual master, his influence in this world is felt through the dream world. A radio station may be far away but its contact with a house radio is made through an antenna at the house of reception. Similarly human beings are directly affected by the spirit world, through psychic transmission and dream contact. No matter the level the spiritual master reaches, he has to make certain that his transmission reaches the dream level from where it affects the human world.

The ego problem

For spiritual masters as well as disciples, there is the ego, which is natural indeed. The individuality of the living being is assured by Krishna in the Bhagavad Gītā and therefore we cannot abolish it. In some religions like Nihilistic Buddhism and Advaita Vedanta, there is an attempt, at least theoretically, to abolish the individual along with his ego, motives, bad habits, and everything.

The ego or assertive sense is bothersome. It is the cause of anguish. Regardless of whether it is used willfully or unconsciously the ego converts the soul into a focal point for reception of pleasures and pains. Some religious systems advocate the removal of that assertive tendency. The assertive power is converted into a sense of possession on the social plane so that the guru may assume an attitude of my temple, my devotees, my people, my mission, my doctrine, my deliverance of humanity and so on.

Some spiritual masters hide their ego by using the word God to cover all personal acts. They speak of God's mission,

God's disciples, God's temples, etc., while in fact they really mean something of their very own. Despite the hiding, some of the more perceptive disciples realize the deception. Material nature certainly detects it and gradually exposes it.

Some spiritual masters effectively sidestep the ego problem by appointing others to lead their society, side by side with themselves. In this way, they assert themselves to the minimum and continue their spiritual disciplines in earnest. They are leaders part of the time and spiritual aspirants part of the time. They do not get stuck with the leadership role as idols of followers.

The world guru pretense

Some spiritual masters remain in a small corner of the world, content with a few disciples, but many of them get famous and then state that they are world authorities or jagat-gurus. Those who are modest but who are just as ambitious, hide behind a set of followers who glorify them. I once knew a spiritual master who used to write a newsletter of his travels. He assigned one of his disciples to sign the newsletter and issue it. This was a pretence, a cover whereby the spiritual master would glorify himself in the newsletter but he would project the idea that he was glorified by a disciple. In this way, he effectively hid his participation in the build-up of his popularity. Some other spiritual masters create a situation whereby the followers declare them publicly as the most qualified guru on the planet but when asked if they are, the spiritual master tactfully denies it and says that his followers made the acclaim.

Some spiritual masters do not establish their position as head guru of a planet but they may check to see how the public views them. For instance, Jesus Christ used to question his disciples. He inquired, "How do the common people identify me?" In that way, even as great a person as Christ noted human opinion.

Some authorities are of the view that every other teacher with followers should submit. In other words, in the spiritual path there is much ambition, competition and influence peddling. It is reactionary, however, to take disciples whom one cannot liberate. Many spiritual masters accept any person who comes along and is willing to glorify them and be their admirer. Actually if one takes a disciple, but cannot liberate that person, one incurs reactions for misleading the person.

Some spiritual masters who have broad powers, feel that they can liberate every human being. Liberating just one person is such a complex affair that unless one is specifically empowered to free that one person, one cannot do so, no matter what one says or does. So we find that in most spiritual societies, a spiritual master attracts many people who enter his society and then become stagnant. When they approach the spiritual master about their supposed advancement, he makes excuses and covers up the deficiency. He relies more or less on their sense of laziness, their satisfaction in finding a faith they can be comfortable with, a process that will not and cannot free them.

Some spiritual masters firmly believe that their system of religion is so complete that even if they cannot personally liberate the disciples, the Deity of the religion will or the process surely will. They hold on to this conviction, do or die, even if it fails miserably in the lives of followers.

Once a spiritual master decides to accept a certain person as a disciple, the consequential equations of the person's previous lives are presented in various circumstances and the spiritual master, if he is able, must work through those challenges of destiny with the disciple. But some spiritual masters mainly tell the disciple to forget the past and focus on the given process. However, the past does not forget anyone and it motivates the disciple repeatedly to leave the association of the spiritual master. Providence presents life situations which are challenging and baffling to disciples and spiritual master alike. Unless the spiritual master can deal with these circumstances and effectively instruct the disciple, there will be no liberation. But the disciple and the spiritual master may convince themselves to the contrary. Many spiritual masters and their disciples live a sort of hope-aspiring dream idea of a liberation that has validity in their minds only.

Two types of spiritual masters

Two types of spiritual masters feel they are world gurus, namely, those who feel there is no God and those who feel there is a God. Among those who feel there is a God, one type feels that God is a person and the other type feels that God is the sum-total reality. A spiritual master who is theistic and who feels that there is a God, may hold the view of himself as the singular or most important of God's representatives on earth.

But no matter what a spiritual master does, says or professes, material nature is in a sense his immediate authority. The limited souls are closely related to material nature as its energizers. Nature does not easily release any limited being. To release one single soul from the shackles of material existence is an extraordinary feat for a spiritual master, what to speak of releasing a sector of humanity. Material nature is so tightly interwoven in human nature that to gain release for one disciple, a spiritual master has to apply all power and more and still he will find that the disciple confidently continues to rely on material nature.

No one is freed by wishful thinking or by the strong conviction of a spiritual master. One gains freedom only by effective proven techniques which are applied in each individual case with precision. Otherwise, the idea of salvation is simply a fallacy.

A spiritual master who is eager for success and who gathers many followers around him will invariably be blind to the hazard of having many followers. The first hazard is that his involvement with so many people will decrease his spiritual discipline. There is only so much time in a day and so much energy in the psyche. A spiritual master who has many disciples must either forego personal advancement for some time or appoint others as substitute teachers.

Getting to power, becoming a leader of an organization, having everyone look up to you and glorify you, is a dangerous achievement for any limited being, even one who professes to be a representative or servant of God. Pride is always present in the psyche. The moment a spiritual leader forgoes his spiritual advancement, and takes the success for granted, his pride in himself and the accomplishments which surround him, go to his head. Then he makes many mistakes, declares many statements that he cannot substantiate. He says many things that will be proven falsities in the course of time.

The disciples of a spiritual master who specialize in glorifying him and who encourage him to think that he is the greatest person who ever walked on earth, do their spiritual master great violence by the flattery they award him. The disciples usually do not understand how they set the stage for the ruination of the teacher.

When a spiritual master is overtaken by destiny which approaches him in the guise of world-wide fame, he is in a dangerous position but most spiritual masters do not understand this. Fame implies that one will lose objectivity and be carried away by composite energies coming from all types of favorable and unfavorable personalities. We see that many politicians are ruined as soon as they become famous, and spiritual masters are spoiled in the same way. The whole idea of fame indicates a lack of control of destiny. In other words, as soon as the spiritual master becomes renowned, he loses control of his bureaucracy but still he might be expert in the pretence of leadership. His loss of control is shown by the numerous senior disciples whom he must appoint to control his assets and to direct his numerous disciples. Many of these seniors do not get his personal touch because he is limited and cannot possibly be in all places at all times. As such, some spiritual authorities take resort to sending books, videos and other media to keep their followers in touch with their energy in one way or another.

Being dependent on senior disciples, the spiritual master must of necessity allow these men some freedom of action. However, in resentment, those who desire the spiritual master's direct association, file complaints against these agents. Gradually various factions develop within the parent society. Then all of a sudden, there are disagreements which the spiritual master tries to settle with veto power.

Many of the problems cannot be settled fairly because the spiritual master has to consider his overall plan. In some cases he must give in to wealthy followers to acquire financial support. And he may submit to a politician if he needs political support. There are variables that come into play once a spiritual master becomes world famous. People hound him down, and because he has so many desires, he becomes a pawn of many powerful or skilful human beings whose services he must bargain for to get help to fulfill his desires and to increase the fame. These, of course, spoil the life of the guru and of his sincere disciples, but neither the master nor the disciples may realize the danger.

Apart from all this, some of the senior followers of the spiritual master will be his enemies in disguise, but he may not realize it. In other words, many persons who end up as senior men actually grow to dislike the spiritual master. They secretly disagree with many of his decisions but they patiently wait for him to leave his body and then they show their colors by declaring themselves as the next competent authority. They sabotage the original intent of the teacher.

Any disciple has desires from past lives, but a spiritual master, like a blind parent, may not understand this, as he may be too caught up in the quest for fame, in being an authority, in being a figurehead and in being someone whom others admire. A parent, for instance, usually does not consider that his child has many lives stuffed into his nature and many corresponding desires. The parent hopes against hope that the child will turn out in a certain way. Similarly the gurus, most of them, feel that the disciples will do exactly as desired. This, of course, is a big illusion in the mind of an authority. Every spiritual aspirant is individual and has individual desires. Usually the living entities cooperate with one another only in disciplines when pressured by providence and they enjoy together in pleasures when socially convenient, but a spiritual master gets the feeling that his disciples love him above anyone else and so he is fooled by sentiments. A parent also gets the idea that he is the only parent for all time and that his child loves him dearly.

In India, there is a standard tradition whereby one regards the spiritual master as the eternal authority, or as the spiritual master from all past lives. In other words, one is supposed to think that the spiritual master of this life was the religious teacher in all previous lives but actually this is more or less an approach and not a fact. One should approach a spiritual master just as if he were an eternal authority because that is the only way to get along with him and to get the best out of him. From the view point of a student the teacher has got to be the only teacher; otherwise, the student will be defiant to the teacher and will not get the best teaching.

Many spiritual masters flatter themselves upon their disciples as eternal gurus while in fact, they cannot explain how it is that some of their disciples came from other religious groups where they accepted a spiritual master in the same way in this very life, while others leave and adhere to other teachers. Therefore, the spiritual masters are many and we accept one after another under pressure of destiny. This does not mean that there is no specific spiritual master or that there is not an eternal guru. Actually there is, but it is still foolish and arrogant for a spiritual master to feel that every disciple who accepts him is an eternal student. It is simply arrogance in the nature of the guru that makes him feel like this.

A limited spiritual master cannot possibly keep track of numerous disciples through all their transmigrations. Therefore, when he conveys that idea, he is being very untruthful. The spiritual master has his own problem changing bodies, getting himself in order, maintaining purity and empowerment, so how can he be that totally concerned about anyone's spiritual advancement? It is simply a farce. Perhaps he can be concerned about one or two souls who are close to him, but not others. The others will be left by the wayside when the spiritual master has to leave his body and fend for himself to recover lost purity, lost sense of direction and weakened empowerment.

The fact that the spiritual masters have problems changing bodies is directly evident by how they are carried away by waves of fame and how they lose control to certain senior disciples, as well as how they have to stoop to rich and politically-successful people.

Let us take for example a certain spiritual master who was born in India. He took birth there in a family of religious authorities. He had the advantage of a youthful life in the house of advanced souls who trained him. He was equipped with all that is required to show oneself as an empowered entity. Still he may find that the people of India do not care to hear him. They have seen a thousand and one descendants of saints. They are not amazed to see another.

To them, every spiritual master is just a master. They are not fascinated. The teacher comes to the United States. When he arrives here, a wave of fame strikes and carries him away. So there, he took a body. He had to change countries just to get a following.

Once he acquires the following he will discover that most of the followers who are willing to glorify him and carry out his order, are unfamiliar with the Vedic way of honor. So now he has to painstakingly train them. After training them, he might discover that the training does not stick. In India where the culture is compatible, no one wants to follow him. They see him as just another yogi, just another devotee, just another mystic, just another transcendentalist. So there he is, baffled by providence in that it sent his following from previous lives into Western bodies.

Now he has to attract them, compromise most of his original ideas, and make one adjustment after another until his mission is different from what he originally intended.

The disciples of such a spiritual master who are successful as leaders in his society are not always fully supportive but they might expertly hide their disagreements and wait patiently for his departure. Then they manifest deviant ideas. While the spiritual master is alive, they realize the necessity to comply with him to become just as famous as he is and to learn from him how to win friends and attract and control followers. Once he is gone, they no longer need him. It is just like a wealthy father whose sons cooperate with him to the greatest extent while he is alive and the business and money are flowing, but as soon as he departs they fight court battles to divide assets and take their allotted portions of the inheritance.

The fame-crazy spiritual masters might forget these ways of human nature but human nature persists. As soon as there is a chance, these realities become evident. Then other followers are baffled. They form factions to fight on and on in an endless array of discord which does nothing but curtail everyone's spiritual advancement.

Fame is so dangerous in the life of a spiritual master that it induces him to think that he is more powerful than he actually is, that he can take on more disciples and handle more contamination than he is capable. Once he becomes carried away, he ruins himself and the mission. Fame should be handled with great care by any spiritual authority. One has to be reserved enough to maintain purity, increase transcendental experience and still function as a figurehead.

False promises of the gurus

There are many false promises of the gurus which pass under the name of necessary slogans to attract the masses to religious principles. Most of the empowered spiritual masters come down to introduce moral principles, not to save the conditioned beings. Most of these gurus simply do not have the energy needed to counteract conditioned existence. The plain truth is that most of them cannot liberate even one disciple. There is so much energy involved in liberating any conditioned being, so much negative emotional energy to eliminate, so many consequential accounts to be settled from previous lives, that it is near impossible for an empowered limited soul to free even one conditioned being.

One tactic used by the gurus to introduce moral principles is to state that they will give ultimate salvation. As soon as the conditioned beings hear that they will gain ultimate salvation, they usually come forward in the hope of getting an ease from suffering. They are mainly concerned with finding comfortable or pleasure situations. They are not concerned with the disciplines required for psychic focus and purification. The idea of the conditioned beings is to find freedom from all sorts of physical, mental and emotional discomfort, but without undergoing the austerity required for purification. This, of course, is an impractical idea, but the empowered spiritual masters must, by necessity of human nature, play along with it to a degree. Subsequently they must promise some type of fantasy-happiness for the conditioned being. They must give some concession for immediate enjoyment. Their actual mission is to introduce moral principles which mean social discipline but since the conditioned beings are not fond of discipline the spiritual masters hide the discipline under the cover of a talk of enjoyment or bliss. Actually they have no intentions of providing one drop of enjoyment because they know very well that it is the enjoyment itself that keeps the souls time-bound. Still by necessity, they give an allowance for some spiritually-destructive enjoyment and the conditioned souls come and join their society, thinking that salvation is easy to accomplish, and that it is attained by a happy process without discipline.

The conditioned beings have many consequential involvements to settle. This will take many lives even if they are to be liberated within a short time, but the spiritual masters hide this truth and tell them that they will be liberated in this life. We see this kind of proposal in Christianity, where a preacher gives the congregation the false idea that they will be liberated in Christ's association in some heaven at the end of this life. Actually there will be no such liberation because they do not qualify for it. Their natures are not purified enough now nor will they be purified all of a sudden at the time of death merely because they believe in Christ's intention to save them.

If the spiritual master is to have any value, he must help the disciple to solve out all the consequential equations. No one becomes liberated by leaving a backlog of his or her bad energy in the universe. Each soul has to settle up personal accounts in one way or the other and the only way to make a summary settlement is by self-reform. Merely belief, mere calling on the name of God will not liberate anyone. One can call on the name of God and when God answers, if He answers indeed, one has to take His instructions for the austerity stipulated for freedom.

Some spiritual masters give formal initiation in a ceremony and make salvation promises. However, after the ceremony, converts discover that they have not changed. For the most part, the ceremony gives some official status as a member of a certain society, as a part of a certain clique, and a sense of status as belonging to such and such a guru. It does not in most cases improve one's character.

We make vows in the ceremony but the ceremony itself, does not change the inner nature or alter the bad character. Most of us continue with the same bad habits. The vow to adopt a life of higher moral principles might change us, but only if we are sincere, only if we apply steady pressure on ourselves to change and only if the spiritual society does not make use of our bad habits. After all, if I used to cheat people financially, and my spiritual master then asks me to go out and acquire money, I am bound to use the old habit. Will he object or will he take the money and stretch his hand for more?

The treatment given to householders

Traditionally in India, householders live apart from the temple and go there to assist in services on certain days but in the Western setting, we find that the Indian spiritual masters take the risk of having householders reside in temples. When they do this they face a problem of regulating the sexual indulgence of the married couples. Actually a sannyasi or renunciant is a person who wants to curtail sensual life, to cut down drastically and since householder life facilitates emotions, renunciant life is contrary to it.

Generally, renunciant lifestyle is alien to that of a householder. In any case, the renunciants need to have some association with householders. Householders run the world. Renunciants rely on householders for financial security. In some spiritual societies, there is a recommended minimum percentage of income that a householder is supposed to contribute. For instance, in Christianity, there is a tithe system where one should give at least ten percent of income but in some Eastern spiritual societies, one is told to part with fifty percent. Whether this is reasonable or unreasonable is not the subject of this book but it is a fact that the renunciants see it as their duty to squeeze money out of the householders. If possible they cheat the householder by offering various so-called life membership or guest house privileges. Many of these programs are old tricks used by monks in India over the centuries to pinch the wallets of householders.

On the other hand, the householder also tries to trick the sannyasis by associating with them to pass off attachment energies. A householder usually has to exploit others in the discharge of his life. When he becomes overburdened and depressed he finds a holy man for relief. This means passing resentment energies to the holy man. The ascetic in turn, tries to make the householder compensate for the association. In either case, a cheating attitude is shared. The householder wants to come to the renunciant and take blessings in the form of energy for success in business, ease of family problems, ease of legal difficulties and dispersion of cultural harassments, while the sannyasi wants to meet the householder to spread influence and acquire funds.

Jokes as spiritual happiness

Some spiritual masters specialize in amusing their disciples with jokes. They convey the idea that the laughter and happiness resulting from such jokes is spiritual happiness. Some others give their disciples excitement in the form of criticism of opponents. The disciples have a good time listening to cutting, critical remarks but these aspects are more or less a cheating method used by spiritual masters who are politically motivated and who exploit disciples and do not give them spiritual life in the form of purification and techniques for salvation.

The disciples, however, do not realize that they are being conned. They do not understand that the master stalls for time and fails to deliver them from the tyranny of mundane passion and ignorance which surrounds the embodied beings. Sitting around a spiritual master, listening to his criticisms and not making any advancement, not seeing one's fault, not improving, not even recognizing that one needs to improve, does not take one a step closer to salvation. It does make one feel self-righteous. It gives a false sense of confidence which leads nowhere in the long range.

Initiation ceremony as a trick of the trade

Each of the spiritual masters has some procedure for certifying disciples in varying stages. At first when one meets a spiritual master one usually gets little direct association, but in the case of a spiritual master who is unknown, he may deal with one personally, cordially, and kindly. Once a master becomes famous and has a bevy of disciples around him, he becomes difficult to approach unless one is plain lucky, wealthy or has political importance.

For instance, if one is the prime minister of a country, a spiritual master who needs popularity may be anxious to meet one. If one is known as a millionaire, a needy, poor spiritual master will be anxious to meet one. On the other hand, a stroke of destiny may arrange for even a poor person to meet a spiritual master of repute and gain insight through the association.

Some spiritual masters set a standard fee and a standard rule of discipline but on occasion, this may be waivered for certain applicants. However, usually the spiritual master will see to it that most people come up to the standard requirement and better yet, the spiritual master will remain distant and allow an agent to do this. That agent will be more than happy to stipulate, "You must do this. You must do that if you want to be initiated by our guru."

Once a spiritual master becomes famous, he usually begins to plot and scheme to influence others to do exactly what he wants. In the unknown stage, the non-famous stage, most of his desires were bottled up for he was kept under lock and key by providence, not knowing in the least when he would get a break or when he would fulfill his heartfelt wishes. In the fame stage all desires run amuck like rain and wind in a monsoon. Then the guru pressures disciples to fulfill desires. It reaches a crisis stage where the spiritual master begins to make huge demands.

At the same time, the newcomers must agree to act as hands and legs, mouths, ears, eyes, and noses of the spiritual master. They must agree to honor him, defend him, praise him and do whatever he desires; otherwise they are barred from initiation. It all depends on how desperate they are to be accepted by him and to become known as his followers. And the more famous he gets the more demanding and arrogant he gets because that is the way of human nature.

In the early life of the spiritual master when he is little known, he gives the best care to disciples and he is most considerate. He has the time to take care of a few followers. He wants to be sure that everything is done correctly in a particular way. When fame hits, he drops this genuine concern. After all, he is only one human being. He can only do so many things at one time. He must now depend on many agents who may not execute his instructions efficiently. Thus he will be shuffling instructions to them daily trying to adjust their shortcomings.

His interest in spreading the mission, in becoming famous, in making his mark on the world, in proving himself to opponents, will foreshadow his interest in the individual development of each disciple. He will lean more and more on a general procedure which does little to solve the individual puzzles in the lives of each follower. Still, he will assert that salvation is assured, provided people agree to serve his mission and fulfill his plan. What really takes place, however, is that the disciples use their life in his service. Some are benefitted by this. Some are stagnated by it. Some merely turn sour, feeling neglected, used, cheated, and rejected. At this stage, the spiritual master becomes interested in increasing the number of disciples. Instead of helping to strengthen followers, he simply pressures everyone to go out and convince people of the power of his process and the saving attributes of his society. Those who cooperate fully and fulfill his desires are promoted rapidly. They emerge as senior men in the society. Others are left in a dusty corner of his movement or they gradually go away, feeling that something went wrong in the association.

Some gurus go even further to keep their process under lock and key. Some of these spiritual masters develop correspondence courses; some develop seminars and charge prices that are quite unreasonable. In any case, they spoon feed their technique or process gradually as one is able to pay the various fees, render the various stipulated services and take on the various types of intimidations.

Gurus who are kind-hearted in the beginning, quickly learn that disciples come, take the techniques and go away without paying or rendering services. Thus they become hard-hearted and set up a system of checks and balances to make certain that they get a certain amount of service, a certain fee and a certain amount of mandatory honor.

In some cases, when one goes to see such a spiritual master, one is barred by an agent who informs that one must have an appointment. When one goes for the appointment, one has to wait for some time, and then one is allowed to see the guru for five or ten minutes. A donation is expected. While one waits the guru seats himself behind an elegant desk where he can look down on the approaching disciples, thus giving an air of authority, seniority, and divinity.

The general attitude of each guru is that if one does not follow the particular process, one is doomed. Therefore, it is a matter of realizing whether or not one needs the process given by a particular teacher. If one does, one has to decide whether or not it is worth the price stipulated. Sometimes, however, one is attracted to a guru but cannot figure out the process mastered by him. But later, upon payment and receipt of the process, one might discover that it is completely worthless, or simply useless for one's advancement. These risks are involved when dealing with gurus. In some cases such risks are unavoidable on the spiritual path.

Convincing disciples that only their spiritual master can assist them in spiritual life

One major fault of a spiritual master is the arrogance of declaring or indicating that no one else can help the disciples. This trait of a spiritual master is similar to the human trait whereby one feels that God alone should help one. In other words, a human being feels so important, so special, that God should directly rescue, advise, and assist. When people go guru-hunting they are usually attracted to an authority who advertises himself as being the one and only effective or potent authority in the world. Some spiritual masters hide themselves by pretending that they are not like that but when it gets right down to it, most of them are exactly like that, feeling that only by their mercy can one be delivered from material existence.

We have already seen the demonstration of this in Christianity, where it is declared that Jesus Christ alone has access to God and Jesus Christ alone can rescue humanity. In Islam we are confronted with a similar premise, that Mohammed is the last prophet and that is it. But people leave Christianity and complain about its narrow approach and then join a religious movement from the East in which another narrow approach is introduced all over again.

So long as human beings are proud of species status, so long as we feel that we are special personalities, this cheating process will continue. It is an endless process that transpires throughout history. Even if one human being is able to transcend his nature, millions cannot do so and this approach to religion will prevail. The spiritual masters will keep coming with their idea of themselves as the one and only guru.

As soon as we decide that we are so special that no one but God should rescue us, or no one but the sole, special agent of God should rescue us, we enter a state of deep illusion and we bar the real God from helping us through so many teachers whom He sends. Because we restrict ourselves in a false view we deprive ourselves from being assisted by others. We follow a popular leader even though he does not see to our personal welfare and he only absorbs our energies for his glorification above all else, not actually helping us to overcome deficiencies in character and spirit.

Our human nature is the root cause of our being exploited by spiritual masters who keep us in their association and bar us from taking vital help from others. They exploit our sentiment and keep us blind and stagnant while they flaunt themselves in human society and use us to prop up their faulty process.

A guru who exploits followers, and prostitutes himself, meets ruination in this life or the next. We also hurt ourselves, keep ourselves down. We stagnate spiritually. In addition, we help to ruin the said guru by adding to his false sense of confidence and by reinforcing his self-delusions.

The celibacy trick

An important aspect of spiritual life is celibacy which is twofold. One part, the superficial part of celibacy, the external visible part, is one's renunciation of sexual indulgence or one's agreement to restrict sexual indulgence to almost nil. The other part cannot be attained unless one practices pranayama techniques because the psychic life force lives on air and subtle energy. Only by controlling that, can it be controlled.

There is a rule in India that an adult celibate monk should be accompanied by a celibate student. Both are supposed to be celibate. However, in the case of celibacy, there is static celibacy and dynamic celibacy. Only those who mastered the pranayama process to curb the life force and transmute the semen, are in a dynamic stage. Others from every spiritual society, are in the dormant sexual stage. This means that due to their engagement in other pursuits, their sexual nature is neglected and their sexual desires lay dormant. However, through practice of the pranayama method the sexual nature becomes purified and uplifted.

Most adult monks are in the static stage. Nevertheless, they do get the respect of being fully celibate because this is the procedure in the spiritual community. As soon as one sees a monk, one is supposed to offer full respect just as if he were indeed a full celibate.

Any celibate spiritual master is supposed to train youths in how to be celibate. In other words, students are afforded his association so that they could develop resistance to sexual indulgence, for without such resistance one cannot get out of material existence. Formerly, in India, the elevated, spiritually-aware householders took their sons to these monks for training. The idea is that no responsible parent wants his son to turn out to be a vice-prone, immoral man. The parent takes the son to someone who is resistant so that the son would get some association and training. It may be compared to the modern effort of parents to get their sons university degrees. The parents do not want their children to be at the bottom of the social ladder, making laborer's wages for the rest of their lives. They make sure that the children attend a university to get a college degree to become a professional.

By tradition, a spiritual master in India, be he single or married, would live off in relative isolation. Some of these spiritual masters resided in palaces but they lived simply and served as priests for dynasties. Some lived in cities or villages but lived simply and served as priests at temples. Some of them were householders but still they were sexually restrained, only using their genitals when begetting infant bodies. In other words, those who were single did not have indulgence. Those who were householders had as much indulgence as was required for producing progeny. Thus both were qualified to raise youths to the standard of celibate life.

Parents would get permission from the spiritual master and would send their son to be trained by him. The son would be trained for some years. While being trained, he would also be educated in spiritual and social life. If the spiritual master foresaw that the said disciple was to be a householder he would send the boy to the parents with a message about the completion of education and association. If the boy was not to be a householder and if by psychology and bodily purification or bodily genetic construction, he could be a lifelong celibate, the spiritual master would inform the parents about that as well.

In either case, the spiritual master did not try to make all disciples become celibate monks. Nowadays, many spiritual masters are haphazard. Some try to make as many single monks as possible, even though later many of these fall in disgrace. The modern gurus are greedy for power and influence. They do not care about the personal destiny of the disciple. They would do anything to anyone to keep their image up and to push on their name and fame. They forego the destiny of a disciple and like whale eating sharks they eat up the lives of their disciples in the name of God's mission. As a result, many of these authorities fall down and are then rejected by their parent society, being pushed off in a corner despite years of service. This goes on and hardly anyone is looking at it squarely and assessing its violence.

There is a fear in some spiritual masters that if they allow the disciples to get married, the boys will lose spiritual impetus, become victims of sexual attraction, build up a household and further extend material existence. Under this fear, some spiritual masters do everything possible to shut their eyes to the upcoming destiny of their disciples and forcibly or by some type of artificial pressure or competitive feeling, cause their disciples to remain as single men. Eventually, though, sexual energy overwhelms and the disciple falls to the indulgence level either with a same sex or opposite sex partner.

The question is: How will the spiritual master become famous if he allows the disciples to get married? How will he have sufficient helpers if his senior men take wives? The answer is to be considered by each spiritual master, for it is a matter of concern for their disciples. It is a struggle between that concern and their greed for popularity and extended power.

In the legendary histories there is sufficient cause to support spiritual masters who tilt their disciples away from householder life. For instance, in the episode of the sons of Daksh, two sets of his sons, one set of Haryas and another set of Savalas were thwarted away from householder life by Narad, and Narad effectively liberated them. He gave them a process that worked without fail, not a process advertised that did not produce the promised result.

Daksh wanted his sons to be sex resistant householders who would beget elevated children, but Narad alerted the boys that their father was irregular and that his ideas were not suitable in terms of their desires from their past lives. Narada instructed them in how to become full single celibates. The process he gave them was valid. Thus from ancient times, there was an effort to get as many disciples as possible to remain celibate, but persons like Narad did not plan to use the disciples for fame, honor and wealth.

Still, the modern situation is not all the fault of the spiritual masters. After all, the male disciples struggle with sex attraction. Some are embarrassed by their lack of resistance to it. Some fear the responsibilities of households. As a result, some unconsciously push themselves in the direction of male fraternity, which develops into homosexuality.

The body guards of the guru

Some spiritual masters become so famous and create such a stir and a dislike for themselves that they must keep disciples as body guards. In fact, some spiritual masters always keep men around them who are expert in the use of weapons or expert in martial arts. This is a manifestation of fear.

It is a fact, however, that any person who becomes famous in human society will need protection since fame invokes envy. Some gurus like envy. They like people to envy them, and want others to compete with them and to oppose them, provided they are not harmed physically.

There is a certain type of human being who is irresistibly drawn to a guru who has many enemies. Such disciples are always willing to sacrifice their lives for the guru and the guru in his folly encourages them to do so, saying that they have every right and that since he is God or the most important agent of God, he is worthy of such defense.

A few of these disciples who like to defend their spiritual master, may lose their bodies in the process and then have to scramble around in the astral planes for years to get another material form. The spiritual master is unable to assist them, even though he pretended that they would be liberated. Many others become dried up spiritually because they lose their spiritual goal which was to become purified, self-realized, and devoted to the real God. Instead, they expend their energy in defending a Guru who, because they were dedicated to him, became obsessed with self-importance.

A perfect guru is needed

Our need to find the perfect guru is itself a cause of our being exploited by gurus. Under pressure of that need, we search for a likeable spiritual master. When one is found, we give full trust as if the person is the all-perfect authority. The guru, in turn, is so flattered by the submission that he directs us totally just as if he were that perfect person. One such spiritual master was placed before a court of law for misusing disciples and directing them in many criminal activities. When the prosecutor questioned, the guru pointed out that his disciples committed themselves and asked that he lead them. Of course, this sort of childish answer to the question will not do, but the point is, that one should not be a spiritual master if one cannot determine accurately when to accept honor and when to deny the privilege. One should not become expert in conning people and pretending that one is more perfect than one really is.

The spiritual master may forget his limitations

If a spiritual master forgets that he is aspiring, that he is limited though elevated, if he forgets that he might be degraded again, if he becomes absolutely assured that he cannot again fall to a lowly level, as he was before, his pride overcomes him, and he takes unnecessary risks which lead to degradation.

When the supernatural people want to abandon a man, they merely retract their inspirations from him and leave him to time, which thoroughly makes a complete fool out of him. Thus if a spiritual master becomes arrogant in the face of the Almighty and towards superior souls, he will definitely realize that they abandoned him.

Fame and popularity among naive, simple-minded people makes a spiritual master arrogant. If he takes the popularity seriously and allows it to go to his head, he will forget that he is limited, that he too is aspiring. He may begin feeling that he is supreme. Thus he will begin to order his disciples to do many things which go against the grain of the supreme will.

Such ruination, however, is part of the same mercy energy of God, the grace of the Almighty, for it quickly causes shrinkage of the mission of the spiritual master. It produces distrust in him among followers. That curtails his arrogance. He gets time to think and reconsider. He is again brought into the proper attitude of humility and appreciation. It is ruinous in the broad sense but it is a saving grace in the life of the spiritual master.

When a spiritual master becomes important and gets a group of loyal do-or-die followers, he naturally becomes arrogant. At that time, if one calls him on the phone, one is stalled by a message from a secretary who says that one should call back later. When one calls back, one is told that the guru is very busy talking to an important person. If one writes a letter, the secretary may not deal with the subject of inquiry but states that the guru has just met the most important politician or persons of significance in current affairs. In this way, the spiritual master creates many offenses, just as if he were an arrogant aristocrat. If one goes to see him personally, one is told to wait at the door and after waiting for some time one is given an appointment. But on the day of the appointment, one is told to wait for at least half an hour before one can see the guru. Finally when one is allowed to see him for five or ten minutes, he sits on a high seat like a court judge and looks down piteously upon oneself and gives a speech. When the interview is over, the guru might ring a bell or give a signal to a follower to arrange that one be escorted to the door. In this way, the spiritual master poses as a man of importance and gradually he enters the realm of offensiveness where the supernatural people come in human form, regard his arrogant conduct and ruin him. They do this by withdrawing their power from him. Since he is arrogant and impulsive, he usually does not realize what took place until it is too late. He falls headlong into hellish complications.

There are many legends which describe the protocols of gurus and monarchs. In one story a king named Revat felt compelled to marry his daughter to a great personality. Since he could not find a suitable person on earth, he took the maiden to the celestial residence of a creator-god named Brahma. On arrival, he requested an interview but he was told to wait for half an hour. The god Brahma was in attendance at a concert. As promised he saw Brahma after the stipulated time but he found out that half an hour in the celestial world was hundreds of years on the earthly planet. His and his daughter's existence was shifted to another era on earth, to the time of Balarama, the brother of Krishna. In this case, one half hour delay in a celestial god's residence caused a shift in a person's destiny for many thousands of years.

In the same story, which related other events in the life of Krishna, the god Brahma, came to Krishna's City, Dvaraka. The god was told to wait since Krishna attended other visitors when Brahma arrived. Being impatient, Brahma questioned the doorman, "Why do I have to wait? Bring to Krishna's attention that I am Brahma, the celestial being. I am an important person. I have an urgent matter to discuss with Him."

The doorman, however, took the message and returned telling Brahma that he had to wait. Brahma became impatient. He thought, "0, how disappointing!"

As he considered this, he saw the persons who were visiting Krishna. They were super-creator gods, controllers of world systems which were beyond the imagination of Brahma. He was humbled by the experience. In this case, and that of King Revata, the delay was appropriate. But when a spiritual master assumes an air of arrogance and does this, he ruins himself.

The spiritual masters are encouraged by time, then shrunk down by time, and then squeezed out all together. When they are being encouraged, they enter the success stage, the popularity stage. They interpret this as the grace of God or the manifestation of their divinity to humanity. When they are being shrunk down, they enter the waning stage, the loss of popularity stage, the stage where many of their chief followers turn against them. They interpret this as the hostility stage when they state that their enemies work against them. Lastly they reach the stage of rejection and disgrace where they become totally confused and fumble around explaining to the remaining disciples what happened to ruin their missions and prestige.

This does not imply, however, that these fallen spiritual masters never had any value. They certainly had value at some stage but even at that time, there were impurities of character which they overlooked, which their staunch supporters could not see. And so the impurities combined with the popularity and gradually overtook them.

In dealing with such a spiritual master, a disciple has to be very careful in order to get a valid process from the authority. The disciple has to serve and keep a distance simultaneously. He should not create complexities which place the guru in a position of defense. If there is a tangle between such a disciple and the guru, then someone will suffer, either the guru or the challenged disciple.

There is a legend about a King Nimi, a disciple of Vasisht. Once, the king wanted to perform a ritual ceremony. He inquired of the guru about it. The king felt an urgency, but the guru stalled. Vasisht said, "This sacrifice you propose is not a bad idea. I thought of it as well. However, the time is not right. I must perform ceremonies for the celestial people. Your program should wait. As soon as I complete other obligations, I can complete your ceremonies."

After this, Vasisht, who was a space-traveling guru, left for the celestial places. The truth behind the issue was that Vasisht wanted to patronize the more prestigious celestial people. He pushed the little Nimi aside. King Nimi, on his part, felt an urgency. He did not wait. He engaged another priest to perform the sacrifice. When Vasisht returned and found that the ceremonies were conducted, he was annoyed. He cursed Nimi, who with whatever power he had, issued a countercurse in reaction to Vasisht's pronouncement. As a result, both of them were affected. If one is not careful in dealing with fame-crazy gurus, someone will be hurt in the process.

For one's own safety, one should not challenge a guru, but if permitted to observe him closely, one should see clearly what the guru does which is right or wrong. All the while, one should keep one's mouth shut, stay with the guru for as long as required to get the techniques or process from him and then silently leave his association. It is simple. One should not feel that one can correct or intimidate a guru without consequence. Unless one has leverage, it is dangerous to challenge even a deviant spiritual master. There are higher powers. One should be confident that the guru will be rectified by higher authorities or by crushing circumstances. There is no need to hurt oneself by tangling with an exploitive guru.

Recently, one famous guru arranged to kill at least one man from his parent society, all because the man challenged and threatened to expose the guru's deviant activities. The danger may go to this extreme. Unless one wants to be hurt in the process it is best to leave such a guru to time and destiny. A guru who misuses himself, his mission and followers, along with the name of God, will definitely be ruined. Such a man needs no help to be dragged down. With every deviant act, he lowers himself further, so it is best to adopt the wait-and-see attitude than to try to discipline him.

When a guru becomes desperate to save his face, to save his image, he will do any and everything, hurt or abuse anyone, so one must be careful. After all, such a man is limited. He is human. He is fallen.

Nullification of the laws of nature by a guru

One trick of the trade of gurus is to do something wonderful which shows mystic power in nullifying the laws of nature. Jesus Christ was expert at this. When his disciples were caught in a storm at sea and were scared to death, he showed a total lack of concern by sleeping away in the boat. This itself was wonderful since no ordinary being, unless he is intoxicated, will remain dull or asleep in a little fishing boat that is being tossed hither and thither by violent breeze and the sea. In any case, to show more glory, Jesus remained calm when his disciples called him. They thought the boat would capsize and they might lose their lives. "Master," they said, "there is a storm. Please save us!" And Jesus nonchalantly, without any effort whatsoever, spoke to the sea, just as if he were speaking to a little boy on the street. He said, "Be calm." And immediately the turbulent sea became still. And of course, his disciples were struck with wonder, thinking, "How could he do this?" Then they considered that he must be God. And they thought, "He is so powerful, that even the sea obeys him."

In another case when Jesus encountered a possessed lunatic, the neurotic spirits in the man's body recognized Jesus' divinity and wanted to get rid of him. The spirits then said, "O son of God, what relation do we have with you? Why are you here? Did you come to give trouble?" And Jesus ordered them to leave the man's body immediately, but they asked him, "Where should we go? You are in charge of the world, so where do you send us?" The dysfunctional spirits were asking for a host body to inhabit and Jesus understood their intent. He directed them to enter the bodies of pigs in a nearby field.

So here again it is described that Jesus Christ manifested wonderful power. However in Christ's case, power was never abused. In fact, there is no single occasion of abuse of mystic power by Christ. His divinity was total. His saintly reputation remains intact even to this day.

In modern times we have miracle workers, but people claim that some misuse the power. Jesus Christ, for instance, made much food and bread out of thin air to feed thousands, but he did that in a humanitarian effort, not to produce gold for fanciful purposes. Thus we have to consider the motive, the circumstance, and the intended purpose in order to determine usage or abusage.

Nullification of the laws of nature will certainly bring followers. As soon as it is known that a guru can nullify or did nullify some law of nature, people are attracted, but if he is not careful, he is ruined. The case of Jesus Christ is there. He nullified the laws and after sometime he began to hide here and there to avoid people. Wherever he went people followed because they heard of his mystic power and desired to live under his shelter to avoid the inconveniences that are part of material existence. Gradually Jesus began to avoid the crowds and in the end, the Roman government harassed him, fearing revolution. These are risks in the use of mystic power.

Nullification of social laws

Another trick of the guru role is to nullify social laws. In modern times, this has become a favorite trick of many gurus who come from India and take Western youths as disciples. There is an example in the life of Jesus. Jesus also had some young men following him, some fishermen mostly. At one time, these fellows were hungry but it was the holy day when the Jews were prohibited from manual labor. According to that tradition one should go to the temple and pray, foregoing all other duties. The disciples became hungry. Since they had no organized social life, they went into a man's cornfield, appropriated corn and ate it. They were seen. People criticized and pointed at Jesus. They said, "Why do you allow your disciples to do this on the Sabbath? You are supposed to be a holy man. Why do you allow your followers to break the religious standard?" And Jesus, in his typical cool-headed manner, reprimanded the people. He said, "The observance of Sabbath was made to facilitate man's religious process, not to bar it. My followers are hungry. They are preachers, let them eat."

In this way, Jesus, Lord that he is, conveniently banished a good moral principle just to excuse his disciples. He might have apologized but he did not. In modern times, many of the gurus do this. Jesus did that once in his lifetime while some gurus do this daily.

In the modern setting, if a guru is not willing to allow his disciples to break some moral principles, he cannot become famous. It is near impossible. It is trendy for a guru to sanction a certain amount of immoral acts and present the false notion that such acts are for a higher religious cause. In doing this, the guru takes a risk, since immorality eats away at his purity. A recent example was Rajnesh.

Chapter 9

Attracting Disciples

Acquirement of disciples

Initially a spiritual master tries to select a few important people as disciples. He needs skilled people to form a core group. Once he gets that group, he expands the society. If a member of the core group leaves, the spiritual master looks for a replacement. The core personalities are selected on the basis of skill, quality and compatibility. For instance, a man may be skillful in a particular way but he may have a bad character which neither the guru nor the guru's process can reform. Still, the guru will keep such a man if he needs the skill in the society. A man may have good character but no technical skill and such a man may not be in the core group simply because his good character makes him too touchy when there is a necessity to bend rules. But one such man of good character who is not so perceptive, who is not so sensitive, who is culturally suitable to the times and who is desensitized to the faults, may be selected as a public relations man or secretary for the society. In that way, people are selected. In other words, in a spiritual society, many people are put into authority who have little genuine spiritual interest.

Once the core group is formed the spiritual master has to develop his plan to expand which means that he has to get a great number of disciples. Certain agents of his will then sit with him and plan programs for luring the masses into joining the society. This sort of approach is standard for many spiritual masters. At the initial stages there is some genuine concern to capture people who can be assisted by the process and association of the society. But later on as the society expands, this feeling is lost and the guru begins to talk about the number of disciples and the greater number he intends to have. He finds that people honor him simply on the basis of a large following, on the basis of numbers and not on the basis of quality of training received from him. Therefore, to expand the popularity, he will encourage his followers to make many converts.

The only way this can be done is to water down the disciplines. As soon as the disciplines are relaxed and the senior men learn to lie convincingly about the process and the result that the process yields, they get more and more followers, until the time comes when the society ceases to expand. Criticism will then come from every corner, and legal or social complications result.

Once the disciples increase, the spiritual master may look around him in an assembly hall and view a sea of eager faces. Then he feels very happy and powerful. This is, of course, human. Any man who can sit around and see admiring faces about him, all enthusiastic and ready to die for him no matter what, is bound to feel some elation. After all, at the core of the personality, a guru is human. A spiritual master will become proud. This is the point at which he envisions world supremacy. At this point he is finished; at least in the terms of his destiny. At this point, he is fixed in the misconception of himself as a somebody. However, material nature and the supernatural people and the real God Almighty might well disagree!

Capturing politicians

In all actuality, a spiritual master of worth is not supposed to stoop to a politician, but in the practical world of spiritual life, the spiritual masters do stoop. It all depends on their strength of austerity, their degree of empowerment and their clear or confused understanding about the supreme will. For the sake of fame and popularity many gurus feel that a little bending there and a little leaning here, is harmless.

The attraction to politics is based on a two-fold factor, one being the power of politicians over the masses along with their control of taxes and resources and the other being the spiritual master's conscious or subconscious memory of his former lives as a politician. If he was a politician in previous lives and if he used to manipulate human beings for political purposes, he is irresistibly drawn back into the political world, first within his own spiritual society and secondly in the general society. He feels that the politicians are misleading the people but he forgets that he was once a politician and that perhaps he is still a politician deep within. As a last resort, he thinks that if he could convert all politicians, the entire world of villages, towns, cities and countries would easily come under his control.

The effort to convince politicians, however, is usually a lost effort because politicians are the most slippery and elusive human beings and while being used by a spiritual master, these statesmen use the spiritual master in turn, in a mutual display of manipulation and power. The politicians have no intention of surrendering their hard-earned power of previous and present lives. And the spiritual masters only compromise so far as they feel able to twist the politician in a certain direction. Eventually there is a cancellation of power as the two clash, debate and then withdraw from each other, with the politician going back to his town hall and the spiritual master returning to his temple or church. As the Western people so emphatically proclaim, church and state should not be joined together.

One theocratic nation where church and state were unified under the power of the religious leader was Tibet, but despite factual complaints about the atrocities of the Chinese Communists under the great Chinese ruler Mao Tse Tung, the fact remains that modern history has carefully and efficiently abolished the idea of theocracy. Practically all spiritual masters who came out of India to the Western countries have tried to establish some sort of absolute rulership of community. They have all been ruined or frustrated in one way or another.

In the ancient Vedic setting, there was never any such thing as a state run by a spiritual master. The confusion in the minds of the modern gurus occurs because they do not understand a simple fact: Many spiritual masters of the past were saints. A saint does not take the role of a political leader unless he first agrees to lower himself to that status.

The modern spiritual masters usually play a deadly game, that of being politicians and that of being saintly, gentle men simultaneously and in a sense this is their fault. As a result, history opposes them and brings their missions to ruination.

Apart from the spiritual views and the fantasies about world control, these spiritual masters keep on dreaming without ever realizing that they have little power. The true world picture is one of control by the mercantile people. It is obvious, if we look at world history today, that the mercantile people are in control. They control the politically-minded people who must bow to them and get funds to sponsor political campaigns. Even after getting a rulership position, politicians must stoop to get bank loans and funds to endorse social programs. The spiritual masters too, must humbly submit their missionary plans to these mercantile people to get donations for their non-profit organizations. Or they indulge in illegal schemes like importation, sale and distribution of narcotics or other such tricky business which causes legal difficulties and disgrace.

As far as the common people are concerned, they are fully controlled by the mercantile people who open large department stores which are flooded with cheap goods. The entire world is directed by the enterprising mercantile people.

In the present era, it is simply not possible for the spiritual masters to run anything because the atmosphere is not conducive. Time is not on their side but still the spiritual masters are dreaming. And the disciples, naive and simple-minded as they are, follow.

Capturing celebrities

Some spiritual masters get the idea that if they could capture a famous musician, movie star or entertainer, most or all of the celebrity's fans would join the religious group. Such spiritual masters arrange to meet a famous person in hope of a full conversion. For instance, in England in the 1960's the Beatles showed some interest in Mahesh Yogi's meditative process. The yogi who was relatively unknown at the time, became famous overnight on the basis of contact with the Beatles. His books, pictures, philosophy and way of life flashed in all news reports all over the world.

There are other examples, but this particular method sometimes backfires on a guru. If, for instance, the movie star or pop idol dies from a gunshot wound or from an overdose of narcotic drugs, the guru's name may be affiliated. He may lose the respect he gets from morally-inclined people. He may also attract hostility from conservatives who feel that celebrities promote vice.

The influence may flow in two directions also with the guru being influenced by the film star or musician. Early in 1994, a British pop star named Boy George who is a noted homosexual singer, began to recover some of his fame which was lost when he became gravely addicted to heroin. Thereafter, Boy George held a press conference before doing some musical tours. He explained that he believed in Buddhism and Hare Krishna philosophy simultaneously. He wore some signs of the Hare Krishnas along with his trademark feminine look. In that way he tainted the Hare Krishna situation. Thus when a spiritual master goes after a pop star, he runs the risk of having the influence flow in the other direction, whereby his society might be damaged in the eyes of the public due to affiliation with a notorious celebrity.

Pop and movie stars are usually wealthy, at least during their popularity phase. Some spiritual masters court them sufficiently to milk them for large donations for a building project, missionary activities or media publications. However, such money is contaminated with negative vibrations. If the spiritual master is not careful or powerful enough, the energy enters his nature and then penetrates the vibration of his society and causes havoc. Eventually the thousands of dollars he received becomes a source of frustration.

For many youths, there is a connection between the taking of narcotics, listening to pop music and submitting to a guru. Some spiritual masters try to deny the connection. Some state outright that drugs have nothing to do with it. But many who flock behind a guru are people who were hung up on drugs in their youthful years in high schools and colleges.

In the developed countries the souls who broke away from Christian influence and Western tradition and who became hippies or other types of defiant youths, did so mostly through drugs and not through reasoning or proper reflection. Some spiritual masters like to think that these followers just all of a sudden began thinking that they should give up materialism. But the truth is that they did so after the so called doors of perception were opened by taking hallucinogenic drugs like LSD or narcotic herbs and drugs like marijuana, heroin and cocaine.

These drugs allowed the said persons to recover themselves in terms of knowing that they had past lives in India and that their Western birth was merely superficial. This writer does not advocate the use of drugs, but in all honesty, the effect of drugs cannot be overlooked.

The value of the pop stars is that they encourage youths to reject tradition and materialism. When the youths do this and are rejected by their disappointed parents, they run to the Eastern gurus for affection and assurance. In the mean time, their parents cry out that they are being brainwashed or kidnapped by Eastern gurus.

The truth of the matter is that these youths who chase after the Eastern gurus are souls whose transmigrations in their most recent lives were in Eastern bodies in India or another Asiatic country. Thus it is natural that they return to an Eastern belief.

By drug use, they suddenly and drastically realize that they are not compatible to Western society, but since they were already indoctrinated in Western ways, they became defiant and irresponsible. Their parents, however, being unaware of reincarnation, do not understand that the said children were souls coming from a foreign culture. The gurus from India are aware of this.

Many pop stars are souls who came from previous births in India or Asia and therefore, they are also attracted to the Eastern religions and create music with an Indian tilt. This illustrates the complexity of destiny.

The hippies rebelled against the highly organized Western civilization which is a natural outgrowth of Greek and Roman history. They rebel because in the previous Asiatic setting, governments simply did not wield such rigid control. Their subtle bodies want freedom from such a society because they were not adjusted to Western culture in their past births in Asia. Still, the Western society proceeds and Western influence swallows up the Eastern ones.

Many gurus who came from the East, beginning with persons like the famous Vivekananda and Yogananda, all felt that they could conquer the Westerners, but what we find is a battle lost. The fight goes on but the battle is lost by the gurus. The result of this shows by the fact that Western civilization is able to contain the hippies and other culturally-resistant youths.

In fact, many religions are formulated as New Age religions which are merely mixtures of Christianity and Eastern systems, as well as mixtures of hippie ideas and hard core Western views. So the Western civilization appears to be consuming the Eastern influence and taking full advantage of it.

At the same time, the Eastern gurus are moving into more and more modern settings with fancy cars, fancy buildings, electronic gadgets and the like. With one part of their mouths, they speak against these things and with another part they call the various companies to order these things.

The gurus pretend to have the divine immunity, in the sense that they pretend that they can mix with Western culture and not be influenced by it. We see, however, that they are being influenced every step of the way. A guru can only safely absorb as much impurity as he can overcome by his austerity. Whenever he relaxes, impurities influence him. Therefore his pretence shows when he becomes contaminated and performs criminal activities, and he becomes proud and blind to his ruination. The whole problem with gurus has to do with the purity they began with, and the continuation of austerities.

As indicated previously, a guru usually does not become purer as he serves as a guru; he either remains the same or decreases in purity. Only if he has the freedom to continue austerities, will he increase in purity; otherwise, he will become stagnant and slide backwards by taking in contamination. We must understand that as soon as the spiritual master takes even one disciple, he has to absorb some contamination from that person unless the disciple is even purer than himself. Usually the disciple is impure and therefore, if the spiritual master takes many disciples, he must become contaminated to a degree even though he will not admit it. His game is to say that he is pure and to convince others that he can handle anything. People usually believe this because they want to believe that the guru is powerful and flawless.

The empowered spiritual master, being a limited entity, must perform austerities to elevate himself. That is the start. Whether he performed these austerities in the present or past life is irrelevant but the austerities must be there because he is a limited soul. As soon as he stops performing austerities, he is in danger unless he can maintain whatever power and purity he accumulated. It is a very simple matter. A vast quantity of water like the sea cannot be exhausted by human beings. It is impossible and the God Person cannot be exhausted, but the limited entities can be exhausted, or become polluted by human usage. A guru is limited and can become contaminated. A guru might flatter himself about being absolutely pure, about never falling down but that idea is flattery only and does not tally with the laws of nature in regards to social involvements.

While he performs austerities he is a disciple and not a spiritual master, but when he stops and takes disciples, he becomes a spiritual master. Now if he stops just a little, continues his austerities and takes disciples simultaneously, he is both a disciple and a spiritual master. Unfortunately, disciples, like children, require some attention at first, more attention later on and then all of the master's attention for the rest of the time. This means that his austerities may be stopped all together. Thus he will become contaminated if he is not able to maintain himself by going into seclusion periodically.

Some spiritual masters take seclusion, and try to recharge themselves again by performing austerities for a time. If a spiritual master is ruined completely just before he passes from his body, we can rest assured that he will take to austerities in his subtle body as soon as he leaves this world. He will more than likely continue those austerities as soon as he takes another earthly form. But the followers are usually not concerned about the balance between austerities and contamination, no more than a child is concerned about his father's income in reference to household expenses. Disciples hardly care. Only the very advanced ones assist the spiritual master with the contamination. Some take it and perform the austerities that would nullify that portion. A grown-up son who is considerate towards a bankrupt father might save some money to help his financially-wrecked parent.

To be a spiritual master and not be dragged down by contamination and one's own impurity in bad motivation, means that one must be a disciple of a higher authority and be a spiritual master for others simultaneously. Both roles must be maintained. One must maintain austerity to please one's authority and also act as a source of inspiration for others. If one ceases the austerities, one will fall down as soon as the balance tips in the direction of the contamination.

Capturing wealth

Some spiritual masters specialize in attracting wealthy disciples. These spiritual masters are of a certain class. They know how to deal with rich men. They do, however, suffer the risk of contamination. There are essentially two risks involved. One is the method of collection of the wealth. The other is the motivation of giving to the guru.

If the rich man collects his wealth in an illegal or exploitive way, the money or the energy is contaminated. When the spiritual master receives it, the contamination is transferred to him. Unless he is very powerful in austerities, he will be affected. If the money is collected honestly, then there is still the risk of bad motivation on behalf of the giver. The bad motivation will affect the guru. Unless he can transform it by influencing the donor, it will enter his nature and affect him.

One such guru had performed austerities in Nepal near the Himalayas. Then he came to the Western countries, and opened his mission which attracted many wealthy followers. He had a particular siddhi, a developed mystic power by which he could touch the forehead of a follower and cause the person to see a mystic luminescence in the brow or crown chakra. Some people used to criticize his use of such power. He called it Shaktipat initiation. By his developed power, he used to transfuse the subtle and gross bodies of the disciples and thus cause these chakras to become energized. As such, his followers became convinced of mystic perception. However, later on, when he passed from his body, he came to the author on the astral level and complained. He said, "Many disciples whom I made when I had a material body were hypocritical towards the disciplines I introduced. They came for power to acquire wealth. They were simply interested in using the developed austerity for attaining money. That is not the purpose of austerity. In that sense, my mission was a failure. I thought that I would convince them of transcendence by energizing them but I got contrary results."

In relationship to the contamination, there is a legend in the Shiva Purana. There was a king named Shatanik who was a very pious man who cooperated with the saints. He used to collected taxes as usual and donate money to the religious heads of his country. As time would have it, he passed away.

When he departed, his son, Prince Sahasranik, took his place. This new king was not as generous as his father. Subsequently, many religious heads left the country since they were dependent on state welfare. Some filed a complaint to influence the King to restore the welfare policy of his father but Sahasranika questioned them. He said, "I heard of the benefits of alms giving. You say that by giving alms to the religious people, a king goes to heaven indefinitely and then returns to this earth and gets rebirth in a powerful dynasty. Since my father passed away, I cannot ascertain his whereabouts. Can you say with certainty where his spirit resides?"

At this, the religious heads hesitated. They could not tell for sure whether King Shatanik was in heaven, purgatory or hell. They had no definite way of proving where his soul went after it left the body. They believed the scriptures just like any other devotee but they could not verify what took place after death. They were embarrassed by the questions of Sahasranik. They avoided him thereafter and searched for a way to show where the old king went.

Later on, they met Bhargava, a yogi saint, who was a capable mystic. They asked him to ascertain where the departed king went but Bhargava was not eager to assist them. In any case knowing that he had mystic vision and authority, they pestered him. He finally agreed to search the hereafter for the departed king.

Taking assistance from the sun-deity in the subtle world, Yogi Bhargava went to the kingdom of the judge of ghosts. This place was far distant in the subtle world but Bhargava followed the sun-god there and finally arrived at a place where there were thousands of hellish conditions for various types of criminal ghosts. As he moved through that dimension, Bhargava heard the wailing of the departed souls. The pitiful cries saturated the atmosphere.

One religious head who suffered there stopped Bhargava. The saint ghost said, "O friend, please pay something for the service I rendered to you before my body died." But Bhargava said, "I am sorry. I brought no money here. Please wait for another time." The suffering brahmin insisted, "No! I cannot wait. Perhaps you do not understand that this is hell. Nothing can be postponed here. In hell a man must pay up immediately or he is punished. You cannot delay the compensation. Pay at once and then go your way."

But Bhargava said, "I cannot pay. O friend, I brought no money. As soon as I return home to the earthly place I will get the proper amount and bring it to you. Let me proceed on the way."

But again the man insisted, "This is nonsense. You cannot delay me. You must pay at once. If you have no money or commodities, then transfer one-sixth of the cultural benefits you will derive in a future life." Bhargava agreed. At this point the merit was transferred to the ghost. Bhargava edged forward to find the old King Shatanika. As he proceeded he was stopped by others. First by a departed dairy man, then by a departed washer man, departed tailor, a departed brahmin and a departed builder all in turn and to each he owed some money for services that were unpaid when they lived on earth. None of them allowed Bhargava to proceed until he agreed to pay one-sixth of his acquired merit. In that way, he donated all acquired merit to counterbalance the obligations. Thereafter, the sun-god led him to the place where Shatanika stayed.

Bhargava was distressed upon seeing the condition of the pious king, for Shatanik's subtle body was hung upside down in a pot and was being boiled. Bhargava, who was wonderstruck at the failure of the religious procedures which Shatanika performed, said to the departed king:

"O ruler of men, what is this? Is this an illusion or are you actually suffering? What about your charity to all those righteous and saintly people? You were maintaining them so they did not have to work like laborers. How is it that your piety was converted into sins?"

The king, who understood his fault in the religious procedure, explained the situation. He said, "There was fault in what I did. I donated alms but the money and commodities given in charity were not earned honestly by me. The money was taken by taxing the subjects. Instead of bringing piety upon myself, I reaped many negative reactions because of severe taxation. Please tell my son that the right type of piety comes from associating with knowledgeable, pious people who actually know the subtleties of compensation. I took advice from ignorant priests. He should listen to saints who understand these matters thoroughly. In the months of Chaitra, on the specified day, he should pray to Deity Shiva, and only use his salary."

Thereafter, Bhargava was released from that hellish place. Returning to the earth, he related his experiences to Sahasranik who introduced a new policy. Money used to give alms to priests was no longer taken from the government treasury. In his spare time, Sahasranika worked as a laborer and whatever money he got as wages, he donated. By observing this austerity, he freed his father from the hellish place.

The point of the story is that money given by a wealthy man to a spiritual master might be contaminated. The spiritual master might believe that he can free any type of money from contamination but his belief, even if it is based on a scriptural statement, may not be operative in a particular time and place. We should judge by the result in the mission of the spiritual master. If his mission is ruined, we may conclude that his procedure for taking the donations, was faulty.

In the modern history of the spiritual masters, we are seeing repeatedly that they are not very careful about the legal and illegal acquirement of money but at the same time, we see that their missionary plans are ruined. Sometimes they encounter legal difficulties and have to suffer jail terms and other forms of intimidation. Therefore, we can no longer just believe any and every statement a spiritual master makes merely because he speaks convincingly. We have to go deeper. If the spiritual master is fame-crazy and desperate for success and popularity, his human nature will allow him to miscalculate considerably. Then the laws of nature will act and expose the fantasy.

Some spiritual masters feel that they can use the holy name or their process of salvation to counteract any questionable activity. They feel that provided they are pushing on missionary activities in the name of world deliverance, anything they do is acceptable, and that any amount of money from any source can be used. But providence may not agree to this. In the *Mahabharata*, there is an explanation given by Sanat which contradicts this. He said that just as birds which are perched on a tree fly from it, when they are disturbed, so the good effects of chanting holy sounds, leave a person who tries to exploit those holy names. This is why we find that many spiritual masters are ruined when they use criminally-acquired funds. The dishonesty, their shallowness of consideration, their lust for success and their enjoyment in influencing others to surrender everything to them, contaminates and makes them unholy. A follower may not detect the deviation until the spiritual master is totally ruined.

Capturing the poor

Some spiritual masters specialize in attracting the poor and simple-minded persons. In some cases a spiritual master just finds himself in a particular circumstance whereby he can only attract poor people. Still, such a master needs assistance from wealthy people from time to time. Generally poor people have more faith in religion and in religious leaders. They are easily attracted provided that food and sympathy are given to them. But the poor man is not free of bad motivation. And if he were rich he might be just as arrogant as a wealthy man.

Generally poor people are searching for an ease in material existence to be relieved from a poverty-stricken condition. They are not really interested in transcendence but they feel their faith in God is a junction point between adversity and plenty. Therefore a spiritual master who works with poor people will invariably become involved in building hospitals, educational institutions and in giving them counsel in regulating social enjoyment.

A spiritual master may have his idea about what he wants to do for mankind but he must, by necessity, deal with social problems to a degree, otherwise he cannot be successful. This is why many spiritual masters open feeding houses, lodging places, farms and such services that provide social ease to the distressed, harassed living entities. We cited Jesus who faced the same problems and who had to multiply fish and bread, as well as grape juice, to feed the masses. Eventually, Jesus began to hide from people. He sneaked off to places where they could not find him.

Attracting simple-minded folk

In attracting the simple-minded folk, a spiritual master must either be simple-minded himself or he must scale down his message to suit the taste of the less-educated. People who are simple-minded are not interested in high sounding philosophy. They merely want faith in God and reassuring belief.

The most common of all are the processes of hearing, chanting and singing the glories of the Lord. This is common in both Eastern and Western societies. Most people cannot be bothered with mental concentration, psychic experience and the resulting philosophy and so for them, the means of deliverance is in making appeals to the Almighty.

Getting publicity

Once he secures a core following, the guru tries to increase the number of disciples through those agents. When the disciples increase sufficiently, people take notice of him.

Once the spiritual master feels that people are taking notice, he tries for publicity. This effort for publicity begins very simply as an effort to present his good character and austere way of life to the public. Later on, his efforts for publicity become motivated by his need to be known as a world-famous personality, his need for wealth, and most of all his need to be in a position to influence people and to be considered by them as a final authority.

Some spiritual masters who feel a need to continue their spiritual development, carefully avoid publicity. They try to play a game of hide-and-seek with the public, where they go into seclusion or move to another area as soon as they become famous. In this way, they reserve themselves to complete spiritual practices. Other gurus welcome publicity with open arms even though they might not be able to manage it and even though destiny might well convert their fame into notoriety.

Becoming popular is always a danger to a spiritual master, because the same popularity turns into dire ruination if he is caught in some immoral or criminal activity. However, some spiritual masters feel that they are so pure, so upright, so faultless or so much of a servant of God and an advocate of man's salvation, that they interpret even bad publicity as good tidings. They feel this way until their missions are totally ruined, at which point they are forced to reconsider.

Usually, in the beginning, a spiritual master does not try for publicity but instead he tries to make followers. He does this very carefully. Initially, his main concern is usually to gain the appreciation of others.

CHAPTER 10

Management of Disciples

Paying off obligations

A spiritual master who has many agents or even one or two agents who endeavor for him and help to establish his image as a world figure, becomes indebted to those assistants. At some point, he has to reimburse them.

Some disciples request compensation in terms of spiritual advancement, improved understanding or direct enlightenment by reception of visions or actual spiritual experiences. But many others request high positions in the spiritual society. Some very rare souls request that the spiritual master name them as his successor.

Disciples who perform criminal or immoral acts for their spiritual master also hold him under an obligation. Sooner or later in this life or the next, the spiritual master has to settle up with them.

In compensating disciples, spiritual masters may use tricks of the trade. Such tricks are essentially executed by paying a disciple in any way except that of spiritual advancement. After all, one goes to the spiritual master for spiritual advancement. That is one's idea, so if one performs either moral or criminal services for the master, one expects to get some spiritual advancement in return. If one gets something else, then the whole relationship is spoilt.

Sometimes the spiritual master gives discipline as a pay off. Sometimes he gives a high position. Sometimes he gives a compromise in terms of telling the disciple not to strive very hard, since in any case, salvation is assured. These are, for the most part, tricks of the trade.

A disciple who is compensated in a materialistic way, becomes a burden to the spiritual master. Sooner or later their relationship deteriorates. Such a disciple simply adds to the already existing liabilities of the spiritual master. Their relationship inevitably becomes strained. Even if they intend to get along, providence does not allow it. They depart from one another with hard feelings and misunderstandings, with the disciples resenting the spiritual master for not giving spiritual advancement and with the spiritual master feeling that the disciple is to blame since he got what he really wanted.

In some cases, the spiritual master becomes obligated to a woman disciple who becomes so powerful of a figure in his society that he has to declare her as a prominent leader. Sometimes he becomes charmed by such a leader who then dictates how he should run the society.

Frustrations

Frustrations regarding disciples inevitably occur in the life of a spiritual master just as they occur in the life of a father, who carefully prepares his children for an adult future, but who may become disappointed with contrary results. For a father there are just one or two, three or four, five or six children, but a popular spiritual master has ten or twenty, one hundred, two hundred or more staunch disciples to pester him.

The **biggest frustration** for a spiritual master is the departure from his mission of a well-trained senior disciple. Nothing hurts the spiritual master more, than to lose a well-trained, reliable, capable senior man. But it happens and in some cases, the spiritual master laments sorely and goes into a state of shock. He must also explain the departure of such a man since other followers may harbor doubts about his process and will require an explanation by their teacher about the reason for the disagreement or dissatisfaction of that senior follower.

Some spiritual masters are expert at explaining away the departure of disciples by pointing out real or imagined faults or offenses of such men. Still, the departures create perplexities that bother the most sweet-talking gurus.

The **second frustration** with disciples is the disciples' lack of progress. The **third** is backsliding of disciples who return to old bad habits which were rooted in their life before they met the spiritual master. Since the spiritual master promised that his process would remove all defects, he is cornered when his men become stagnant or when they return to old habits. However, the more intelligent, more conniving, quick-thinking gurus have methods of explaining away these occurrences.

When a senior man becomes stagnant the spiritual master usually uses one of the two processes to get him moving again. The first is insult. To insult such a man the spiritual master usually talks to him in an open lecture in a cutting way so as to damage the man's sense of prestige against lesser disciples. If after being insulted, the man still does not resume the austerities and embrace disciplines, the spiritual master may give the man another position in the society. Sometimes the man is demoted, sometimes he is promoted, but in either case, the motivation of the guru is to get that man moving again since his stagnation affects others and causes newcomers to relax in the process. The first procedure, that of insult, is psychological treatment. If that does not work, the spiritual master realizes that the particular senior man is in a very helpless position. Then the external method of promotion or demotion is used. In some cases, neither of these methods works. The man either stays on in the society callously or goes away never to be seen again.

The **third frustration** occurs when senior disciples fall back from acquired advancement. Senior men who backslide are considered to be dangerous by their spiritual master but if he still has a value for them or if many other followers rely on the person, the spiritual master will call the man up privately and give a firm talk. He may reprimand the man, saying, "I did not expect this of you. Why are you doing this? People complain. It does not look well. Straighten up. Defeat the lower nature. Show the people that you can resume the practice."

Sometimes such a tactic works for a day, month or year and then the disciple returns to the deviant path. Then the spiritual master must decide to keep such a man in a broken-down condition or expel him from the society. In some cases, the man may be very valuable for bringing money or using a skill, so he is kept on for the particular service even though he is not honored as he used to be. He is kept but he is considered fallen. Officially, people offer him honors because of his financial capacity or skill, but behind his back they ridicule him, "This man has done so and so. Even though he was with us for years, he does so and so. He is a rascal."

Some persons who backslide and who have less value are not tolerated in a spiritual society. They are summarily called up by an official and told in no uncertain terms to hit the road. A leader will call such a person and say, "Our leading men insist that you leave this society. Do not associate with us. For that matter, go where you like but carefully avoid us. Do not tell anyone that you were with us."

The **fourth pain** in frustration is the disciples' lazy attitude towards the mission of their spiritual master. If a spiritual master has an evangelistic view of his mission, he will expect most disciples to catch the fever of propagation. They will be expected to go out and preach his message. If they are reluctant, he will feel great frustration. To get them moving he will create incentives such as positions for men who excel in preaching. But, if after creating such incentives, the men are still lazy, the spiritual master will suffer considerably.

The **fifth pain** in the frustrations with disciples is the departure of senior men who separate and then set up their own preaching missions side by side with that of the spiritual master. This is the most painful frustration of all. When a senior man leaves the spiritual master and gets the idea that he can set up his own preaching mission, hang up his own missionary sign and work independently, the spiritual master feels greatly pained. He feels that the man is ungrateful towards him and that potential followers may be drawn to the man.

According to the Vedic tradition, no disciple of a spiritual master should establish any independent preaching mission while the spiritual master uses the same material body. In addition, it is said that one should not even start a preaching mission while any of one's senior, well-standing god brothers are alive. Thus there are stipulations. A disciple who bypasses these rules and regulations runs the risk of being cursed by the spiritual master or by senior god brothers and depending on the situation, the curse may or may not take effect. It all depends on relative potency and empowerment.

It is said that if one wants to have his own disciples while his spiritual master is still using the earthly body, one must offer those people to the spiritual master for formal initiation. If one cannot do so, one may assist those persons in spiritual disciplines without initiating them. One can continue preaching but it is said that one must do it in such a way that there is no need to take formal disciples. Otherwise, one must prepare for a curse or for some sort of reaction.

The spiritual master may face certain complications that frustrate his mission. Until these are worked out, it is said that a disciple should not, under any circumstance, initiate any man but one can give instructions informally. If one violates this, one must be prepared for resentment energies from the spiritual master and offended god brothers.

Unless one is protected by a higher authority, the effort to step away from a spiritual master and to establish a separate mission as an initiating or official authority, will be frustrated by providence. Even if one has the higher protection one still has to act with caution since if one slips in the least, one will be cut to pieces by the willy nilly providence and by the subtle operations of the supernatural people who pass by unseen in the sky.

The **sixth frustration** of the spiritual master with his disciples is the waning of his movement during his lifetime. So long as the movement flourishes during his lifetime, the spiritual master will be satisfied to a greater degree, but if during his life, his mission becomes ruined before his very eyes, he will be frustrated. He will trace the frustration to contaminations brought in by numerous disciples or by certain influential men in his society.

Overall, there are many petty frustrations that a spiritual master experiences, but these six are the main ones. And opposed to these are the successes of the spiritual master.

Grasping their confidence

Being a spiritual master means essentially being able to grasp and direct the confidence of disciples. If the spiritual master is unable to grasp complete confidence of his disciples he might suffer. It all depends on how realized and how humble he is. Some spiritual masters make an effort to grasp all portions of the confidence of their disciples and if they are unable they lament.

It is a fact, however, that in the present era, people usually cannot give all their confidence to any particular guru. This is due to trying times, in which cultural backgrounds of human beings have become complicated. No part of the world is isolated and so from childhood each human being is bombarded by variant values. When one meets the guru, one already has many impressions and views impressed upon the mind. Thus one cannot all-of-a-sudden get rid of these. Some spiritual masters feel that once they hold an initiation ceremony and chant certain mantras in the ear of disciples or give the disciple some process, all past impressions will disappear, but actually this is belief only. In the practical field old impressions may lie dormant for the time being and resurface in the mind at a later date.

Apart from cultural complication in this life, further complications from previous lives are lodged in the subconscious and will arise in the mind of the disciple to pressure him or her in a direction that is not desired by the guru. In addition, social problems from past lives of which the supernatural people are aware, will be presented to the disciples from time to time. Even though the spiritual master will try to banish these or explain that in his religion such things are nil, the supernatural people will pressure and insist that they be solved out by the disciples. Thus the disciple might have to go away from the guru in order to settle up with the supernatural people and with other human beings to whom he or she is obligated by virtues of services received in previous existences.

Those disciples who surrender the most to the guru become his confidential followers and others who are unable, are considered to be outsiders or people on the edge, people on the fringe. In either case, the spiritual master is always aware of the degree of control he has in the life of each disciple.

Essentially there is a power struggle between the spiritual master and material nature for control of the disciple's life. If the spiritual master wins for a time, he might again in the future lose, for material nature will sometimes release a conditioned soul for a few days, a few months, a few years and then reasserts her supremacy in the person's life with greater force, thus baffling the guru.

Once the spiritual master wins the disciple's confidence he feels secure, because being a spiritual master means a fight with everything else, to try to capture some conditioned souls from nature's control. And so the spiritual master feels like a champion if he can completely capture just one personality. But usually nature resumes a strong influence over those who take shelter of a guru.

Emotional disciples are one kind of problem and rational-minded followers are another. Most spiritual masters prefer to have emotionally-minded disciples since human beings are easier to sway if they are emotionally-motivated. There is a greater risk with the emotional-types however, since material nature is more able to recapture them and this pains the guru. As water easily runs down an inclined plane, so the energy of material nature easily runs through the emotional nature of a disciple and captures that person away from the guru for a time or for a life as the case may be.

The rational type of disciple can also be captured by material nature since material nature also works within the analytical process of the living entity. But those who are rational may resist material nature more than others. However, such disciples have the thinking, reasoning tendency and always pester their spiritual master for explanations, checking everything carefully and sometimes speculating about the value of the process he offers.

Most disciples of a spiritual master are attached to the particular type of sense gratification he advocates and not to the austerities he recommends. Therefore there is every likelihood that they will neglect the austerities and indulgently attend to the enjoyable part of his presentation, all to his dismay.

If the balance between the austerities and sense gratification tips in the direction of sense gratification, the society becomes ruined but if austerities supersede, the group is strengthened. The spiritual master is affected accordingly; he is strengthened by the seriousness of disciples and dragged down by their indiscipline.

The spiritual master usually keeps the secret of how contamination is handled. Some masters pretend that they never absorb contamination from disciples, but we can rest assured that the contamination passes anyway. The spiritual master feels it. The issue is how much contamination passes and how much austerity is required to counterbalance it. If for instance, a sex-prone person joins and becomes a disciple, some sexual energy passes into the subtle and gross body of the spiritual master. If he is not a perfect celibate with a purified body, he is affected. He may suppress the affection. He can do so but it will be there regardless. As such, some spiritual masters fall to sexual indulgence after taking sex-prone disciples.

By the same principle if the spiritual master makes a disciple of a criminally-minded person, then the spiritual master might all of a sudden begin criminal activities. Therefore one has to realize that the spiritual master, despite his assurance of purity, may become contaminated.

We can know for certain, that if the spiritual master declares himself as the world's guru, or as having access to the salvation of every man, and if that is not true, if he is actually not that empowered, material nature and the supernatural people will take offense. They will set a trap for him, one that he will never spring out of. As such his mission will be ruined. He will be disgraced in the eyes of humanity.

A boy from India is better suited to taking up a religious process that originated there while if an American adopts an Eastern process, he has to do much adjusting to make himself compatible with Eastern cultural ways. Many spiritual masters from India experience this problem when they come to the Western countries and open preaching missions. The Western disciples who probably had Indian bodies in previous lives, simply do not give up the undesirable Western traits, even though they possess great eagerness to adopt the religion of the previous existence. This is one way in which material nature fights the guru.

By creating an ashram or isolated community in a Western country, a spiritual master tries to ward off the Western values and to institute his own cultural bearing which suits his process. But inevitably he finds that he cannot ward off the Western ways completely. In some cases, his society becomes so westernized that it causes radical adjustments in his process and twists his message and religion in a totally new direction.

Teaching and training

A spiritual master can teach disciples through their conditioning. That is the most rapid method. Whatever cultural affiliation the disciple is attached to, that is the fastest medium of teaching. The problem arises when the religion or process being given by the spiritual master has another cultural basis or requires another cultural setting for proper cultivation. Then the spiritual master has to adapt his process somewhat to suit the new culture. In doing this, he may miscalculate, thus creating defects and perplexities.

Chapter 11

Classification of a Guru

Vision of disciples

The self-image of a guru is more or less determined by the response of the disciples, especially the main disciples who helped in the beginning of his rise to power and world recognition. We must remember that a spiritual master usually starts out as a student of someone else and not as an authority in his own right. After he serves another spiritual master and practices some austerity in this life or the past life, he then begins a preaching mission.

He can only hope for success because he cannot anticipate how providence will treat him. If providence begins to facilitate, he will capitalize on it. Providence and the nature of the followers team up to mold the master in a particular way that may or may not correspond to his original idea.

One thing is certain: If the guru wants worldwide recognition, providence can easily trick him with offerings of fame and glamour. He may be swayed by foolish, naive, slow-thinking followers who offer money or skills for the operation of the society. Many gurus thus fall into the trap of providence and enter a sort of Death Valley from which they cannot escape.

The vision the disciples have of the guru, is important because usually the guru is a limited entity only. As such he is subjected to influence. His resistance to other limited beings decreases considerably once he sees himself as guru because then he understands himself not as an authority but as *the* authority. He becomes prone to taking shelter in the autocratic power which manifests in his group as his command over situations. In his little or large group, he wields the most power. Therefore he becomes like a god to the followers.

Essentially there are three general images formed of a guru. Disciples usually see the guru as:

- ***God in human form***
- ***a perfected human being***
- ***a hero idol***

Other disciples see the guru as a combination of these three. For instance, in Christianity, people see Jesus Christ as God in human form, as the perfect human being, and as the supreme martyr. The Christians say that Jesus is simultaneously the only begotten Son of God and the Son of Man. As far as they are concerned he is the most compassionate human being who allowed himself to be crucified by offenders and yet prayed for their relief.

God in human form

A disciple who regards the spiritual master as God in human form, places full faith in the guru. In such a condition the disciple surrenders everything he has and requests guidance in return. However, the main impetus is the disciple's need for protection from the ravages of material nature. Persons who see the guru as God are for the most part running away from the vicious, exacting, enormous power of providence.

On the other hand, the guru allows himself to be flattered. In this way he takes himself down a slippery course of delusion through which he offends the Supreme Being as well as material nature and human society. As such, if he allows this type of idea to rule his intelligence, if he takes this seriously, he will be ruined. He will see a term of hell definitely. No matter how great a limited being may be, he cannot be the Supreme Being at any time. He can control a small part of a small planet somewhere. Such a man is not prepared for the awesome responsibilities involved in controlling the world much less the universe, but he may want the glory of the Supreme Person who actually has such control.

In fact, if such responsibilities were revealed to a limited person, it would be tremendously frightening. We get some idea about the real God in the Bhagavad Gītā, not in terms of human love, human affections and sentiments, but in terms of the way the world really works, which is the way of struggle of man against nature and God, of puny wills assaulting the divine will, of the Supreme biting, chewing, pinching, burning and doing whatever is necessary to subdue unruly worlds.* This is the real God, not a sentimental human being who has finally reached his peak of world fame and is now hitting the headlines of the *New York Times* or some such paper in a corner of a puny planet in a dimly-lit corner of outer space.

What some limited gurus really want is glory, not responsibility. This is where they are exposed as false gods, gods of nitwits, gods of dull-minded beings.

Now there is a positive side to seeing the guru as God. Some Vedic scriptures recommend the view that one should regard a guru as God in human form since without the guru one cannot reach God. But that does not mean that the guru should take this as a basis for arrogance towards the real God.

---

* *Sanjaya said: O King, having said that, the great Master of yoga, Hari, the God Vishnu, revealed to the son of Pṛthā, the Supreme Form, the supernatural glory.*
Countless mouths, eyes, wondrous visions, countless supernatural ornaments, supernatural uplifted weapons,
...wearing supernatural garlands and garments, with supernatural perfumes and ointments, appearing all wonderful, the God appeared infinite as He faced all directions.
Imagine in the sky, a thousand suns, being at once risen together. If such a brilliance were to be, it might be compared to that Great Personality.
There the entire universe existed as one reality divided in many ways. Arjuna Pandava then saw the God of gods in that body.
(Bhagavad Gītā 11.9-13)

The advice is for the benefit of the disciples so that a disciple can approach the guru with an agreeable attitude. It was never meant to flatter the guru. If the guru misunderstands, he will certainly fall. The same material nature that assisted him, the supernatural people who set into motion the providence of his fame and the same real God who sanctioned his rise to power, will suddenly abandon him.

A guru who props himself up on the world's stage, leaning heavily on the vision of his followers, is a mad man. He got power but lost touch with reality. He may be compared to a man standing on a rotten bamboo pole, who will have a very terrible fall. Such a man is a most pathetic human being, a victim of circumstances.

If the guru has any sense at all, he will allow certain disciples only to regard him as God in person but he will not regard himself as God in person at any time. He will always know that he is limited. To his mind, he is a somebody only because of divine support. He knows that the power he possesses can be retracted. If he forgets that, he will be gobbled up by pride. Then he will be hostile to disciples who do not see him in that absolute way. He will begin to project an imagined supremacy which will ruin him.

Some spiritual masters who fall victim to this syndrome, know very well that they are not God. They are aware of their shortcomings. They know of others who are greater than themselves but they are too small-minded to avoid the temptation. They play God in some small, spiritually-dusty corner of the world among sentimental followers. In this way, they give facility for pride and subsequent fall. For those who follow such a man, there is a lesson being taught. It is a hard lesson but a necessary one. The only way these gullible disciples can overcome their simple-mindedness is to be repeatedly disappointed by such gurus life after life, until they are thoroughly disgusted and honestly seek self-improvement, and thereby attain higher perception and become worthy of a more sincere authority.

Vision of the guru as a perfected man

The vision of the guru as a perfected man also takes the form of the vision of the guru as a perfected servant or instrument of God. This vision is the best vision to have of a guru. It is the best idea the guru might have of himself when he rises to power. But there are flaws in this vision also. An authority in this position might abuse himself and the followers. After all, if one thinks that one is a perfect servant of God, one might get to thinking that one can do anything and everything since one is God's representative. Thus one might perpetrate whimsical acts for which one might be sorry later. Still, this idea of being a servant of God is a better view than thinking that one is God in human form.

The vision of a guru as a perfected man and that of being a perfected servant of God is similar. Before a man can present himself as a perfect servant of God, he must have some self image of himself as a perfect or near perfect man. In some cases a guru gets a vision. In others, he gets an inspiration. In some others he is empowered by his predecessor. In any case, he must have self confidence before he can present himself. If there is no self confidence, he will instead hide and wait to become famous after he passes from his body. A certain amount of courage is required before any person with a perishable body faces human society and presents himself as a perfected human being in the service of God.

This does not mean that the spiritual master will declare that he is perfect. He might speak to the contrary, but within he must have confidence before he can face a proud and doubtful humanity.

Essentially a perfect man must be one who is morally sound in every way. Such a guru must be above question in character and moral habits. If there is some question, if there is indeed a fault which people criticize, he must conceal the fault in order to survive. Most spiritual masters suppress bad habits or flaws in character and proceed. Some courageous ones merely dismiss complaints and excuse themselves.

The disciples who are attracted to such a spiritual master are usually appreciative of his periodical humaneness and humility. They accommodate his dictatorial approach to society. As the founder he is for all practical purposes a god in his society but as a human being he takes the role of a servant and messenger of God.

A spiritual master who starts out as a servant of God will in the process of time shed his role as a mere agent of God and assume dictatorship to human society, telling human beings what they must do for their ultimate good as he sees it. And his followers will threaten human society with statements. They might say, "Our spiritual master alone knows what is right. He alone knows what is wrong. He alone can direct humanity."

Vision of the guru as a hero or idol

Some spiritual masters see themselves neither as God nor as a servant of God but as a hero of a section of humanity, as a current idol without any affiliation to God or anybody for that matter. They see themselves as new persons with new missions and doctrines. They attract followers who are atheists or who have no preset opinion of God and who do not want to see any particular religion on the surface of the globe.

The *hero* **image** gurus take great freedom to create new religious systems and beliefs. Gradually, if they survive the public pressure, they build for themselves an empire of followers. Some of their followers become disgusted and threaten to kill or hurt them. Some others go away and tell amazing tales of their activities. Gradually their situations are ruined.

Disciples who desire a hero idol are not prepared to study scripture in depth or to protect themselves from abuse by a guru. They merely want someone they can look up to, someone they can praise, and some cause to rally around. They are like inexperienced children sitting around a clown or aimless youths around a gang leader or so many fans around a celebrity. Still such situations are a natural development in human society.

Most of the limited entities in the material creation are progressing at their own rate, which implies that they are given broad leeway to make mistakes and to be exploited by others. This allowance is given for the development of different instincts by repeated frustration in time and circumstance.

Collective efforts are there but in actuality the limited entities are freed individually by specialized treatment according to the particular psychological faults they developed in association with material nature in the course of transmigration. Until an empowered soul can rescue a particular living entity, the tomfoolery will go on. Once one soul is rescued, others will remain entrapped, in endless whirls of surges of illusion. Some individual effort is required but essentially, freedom from material bondage means being rescued by a higher authority.

Chapter 12
Special Complexities
of Disciples

Disciples who control the spiritual master

If a spiritual master is not well equipped before he begins a preaching mission, he will, for the most part, depend on disciples for services and skills. He runs into the problem of being controlled by them to a greater or lesser degree. The control of the guru done by the disciple is a very technical matter but the danger is that the desires of the guru are gradually scooped out of his nature and the desires of his key disciples are installed in his mind. In the end, that person who started as the leader or director, actually becomes a stooge of followers, a mere figurehead.

According to a law of psychology, any two personalities who associate will share influence. This influence is shared in three distinct ways: shared discipline, shared enjoyment, and shared discipline traded for enjoyment. This applies to the guru and disciples as well. In any spiritual society the spiritual master has key disciples with whom he feels comfortable. A guru rarely disciplines these disciples. They function as favorites. In other words, the relationship is one of shared enjoyment through similar pleasure taste. This type of disciple is the one most envied by others. While a gentleman has a modest wife with whom he shares pastimes, a guru has favorite disciples with whom he shares jokes, nice edibles, living quarters, travel commitments, public meetings and leisure.

Another type of disciple is the serious disciple who also may want an agreeable relationship with the guru but the guru might keep that person at a distance. As soon as the serious disciple attempts to be familiar, the guru might remind him, "You are my disciple. Why are you treating me like this? If you maintain this behavior, our spiritual relationship will terminate." Typically, a serious disciple gets such treatment from the spiritual master. Actually this type of disciple is in the best position to make advancement. He must constantly give service and attention to the guru.

If this disciple is cool-headed and does not envy the favorite ones, he will make rapid advancement and get the spiritual process of discipline from the guru. This spiritual process of discipline which is usually hidden, is the key to success in spiritual life but the guru conceals it because he does not want anyone to excel at it. If the disciplined disciple can bear the isolation and austerity, he will reach the highest stage. There are many stories in the Vedic literature to support this. Arjuna for instance, was in a disciplinary relationship with Drona who was a military master. At a certain point, Drona began to realize that Arjuna excelled all other students. On one hand he appreciated this. On the other hand he did not. Drona's son Ashvatthama was also in training. Drona was uneasy about Arjuna's genius in learning.

Drona engaged a servant to hinder Arjuna. He told the servant, "Do not serve food or anything to Arjuna during the night. Never offer him anything after sundown. This is an important instruction."

The point was that if Arjuna was handed anything at night he might, through his keen sense of discipline, realize that he could discharge arrows accurately in the dark. Drona knew how to shoot arrows accurately in the darkness, a technique few warriors of the time mastered. He did not want Arjuna to discover the secret.

After this, the servant watched Arjuna and never offered anything to Arjuna in darkness. Later on, however, Arjuna himself with only the help of circumstance, during a meal, realized that his hand could find his mouth in the darkness. He began to practice military arts after sundown. One night Drona heard the twang of a bow string. He surmised that Arjuna surpassed all his students and had moved into the ranks of the most superior bowmen. So it is like that; if one is naturally self-disciplined and plays the game right, one might come up to a high level of advancement.

There is danger, however, in irritating the guru and offending his important disciples. Discipline is good but it can also bring a sudden halt to progression. Drona had a rebel student named Ekalavya. This warrior was an aborigine who took Drona as a spiritual master without Drona's permission.

Since he was as an outcaste he could not qualify for military school just as the son of a poor man cannot go to a great university because his parents cannot pay the required fees and because he lacks formal education to qualify for entrance. Ekalavya formed a clay idol of Drona. He respected the idol just as if it were Drona. Gradually he became expert at using the bow. No one knew about him but one day providence exposed him. The students of Drona were out in the forest on a target practice. They found a dog with arrows shot through the mouth. Examining the dog, the Pandavas understood that whoever shot those arrows was a marksman. They did not like the idea of there being any marksman unknown to them. They searched and found the aborigine. They asked, "Who is your instructor?" The man gave Drona as the name of his teacher.

Arjuna then went to Drona and complained because at one time, in pride over Arjuna's success as a student, Drona promised that there would never be a warrior on earth to compete with Arjuna. Arjuna complained bitterly that now there was another student who was just as good or better. To appease Arjuna, Drona went to Ekalavya. Drona asked the young man who taught him such military skill. In all simplicity as an aborigine, Ekalavya answered, "O master, you are my teacher. Here is your idol form that I respected and worshipped. Through respecting the sculpture, I acquired this skill." But Drona, who was a sophisticated man, replied, "If you accept me as the instructor and if you admit that you got the skill from worshipping my statue, you should pay me a guru's fee." Ekalavya agreed and when he enquired of the fee, Drona asked for the aborigine's right thumb. Then and there, the aborigine without hesitation cut off that finger. And that was the end of his superior archery. A right-handed archer cannot expertly set arrows in a bow without a right thumb.

In that situation, we see that Ekalavya sharpened and displayed his discipline in such a way as to cause Arjuna to be envious and fearful of him. Subsequently his progress was checked. It is like that in the association of the spiritual master. One has to be very careful with fellow disciples, especially with those who are favorites of the guru. If one does anything to arouse fear or envy, one might have to suffer at the order of the guru.

In some cases it is shared discipline in both directions, where a student is disciplined and the spiritual master acts in a disciplined way in the presence of the student no matter what. In other cases, the master is relaxed in the presence of the student but he demands that the student assume a state of soberness in his presence.

Those disciples in whose presence the spiritual master feels compelled to be disciplined are God-sent disciples since they keep the spiritual master in order and remind him of the obligation for austerity and practice.

Selecting a guru who cannot liberate oneself

Selecting a guru is not such a technical matter as it may seem, except for very advanced souls who know what they are looking for in spiritual life. Unless one knows the whole path of spiritual advancement and knows the particular techniques required, one will, of necessity select a guru haphazardly. It is a fact, however, that the guru selected is sent by providence at a particular stage of the disciple's life. The problem is that a disciple might stay longer with a certain master than necessary. Then the disciple becomes stagnant or gets caught up in a power struggle, trying for promotion in a spiritual society which is of no use because one really requires more refined techniques.

Most human beings want an easy-going, salvation-promising, slogan-yielding spiritual master who in truth and fact can hardly liberate anyone. Human beings by nature do not really want complete release from material nature. They desire a one-sided liberation to continue in material existence without difficulty. Leaving aside difficulties and frustration, most living beings are accustomed to material nature and think material existence is just fine. As such they try to find easy-going gurus who assure them that by taking it easy they will be liberated.

Finding a guru who can liberate the disciple is not an easy task because such gurus who are capable of freeing someone from material existence usually hide themselves in the subtle world. They hardly take birth on the earthly level. In fact, the real guru is God. All other authorities are under Him, either to assist Him as described in the Bhagavad Gītā or to frustrate the purpose of the Bhagavad Gītā. No one can liberate another entity unless he is directly sent and empowered by God. If it were an easy task to find a perfect guru, all the aspiring seekers would have found one already and no one would be baffled on the spiritual path. The real gurus as well as the Supreme Being hide from the average seeker. This is due to the bad motivation of the seeker and the seeker's inability to take up needed disciplines. Divine graces are falling upon human society like rain falling from the sky in a typhoon but human beings are resistant. They can hardly make use of the grace due to instability in spiritual progression.

The real path for any particular living entity is not a matter of a general process of liberation. Each living entity is captured and bound in a unique way by material nature. An entity must be released in a specific way. The general paths are only a starting point.

They act as an orientation whereby individual disciples are singled out and treated separately for the peculiar material affections which keep them down in material existence. The knots of illusion are tied in different ways in the hearts of each living entity. As such, particular freeing techniques must be used by the expert masters. In the medical field a man with complications of several diseases must be operated upon by one surgeon specialist after another; so also a disciple may submit to one guru after another, according to the particular freeing-techniques required.

Chapter 13
Envy of the Guru

Admiration

In many cases, admiration of a guru is actually envy of the success of the guru. This envy can be positive in the life of a disciple, if he understands that the spiritual master came to power by performance of austerities through particular techniques. If the disciple feels that it is just the good luck of the guru, he will be misled. If one envies the guru, it is best not to suppress the envy. One should research the nature of it to determine in oneself exactly what one desires that is displayed in the life of the guru. In any case, one has to see that what one really needs is not the attractive results in the life of the guru but the techniques used by the guru through which he came to prominence.

The problem is that most gurus do not reveal how they acquired fame. They carefully hide this. Some gurus honestly forget the technique used because it was performed in a previous life. Nevertheless, if a disciple feels the envy, he can get rid of it in either of two ways, namely by imitating the guru or by performing the austerities for the power by honest endeavor.

If he imitates the guru he will get quick results but people will resent him for it. If he performs the austerities he will get gradual, definite results in the course of time without the resentment taken on by those who try to replace their gurus or set up parallel missions in competition with him.

Envy is part and parcel of material existence and an essential part of our evolution, so there is no sense in dismissing it. We must learn to work along with it in all honesty and be willing to pay the price for what we envy in others. There is no point in trying to dismiss envy because it does not go away by wishful thinking. Due to an impure nature, we have to conquer envy gradually by honest endeavor to acquire that which we envy in others.

To be practical one should train the self to transform the envy of the spiritual masters into envy of his austerities and spiritual disciplinary techniques. If we can learn the disciplinary techniques and honestly apply these, the envy would permanently leave us.

Usually the success is seen and not the techniques through which the success came. Therefore one must watch a guru carefully to understand the techniques. It is just like watching the motions of an expert musician. One cannot learn to play an instrument by watching an expert in concert because he deliberately and unconsciously makes many misleading motions which are not part of the technique required to bring out the sounds but which are part of a show performance.

The gurus act in certain ways which confuse disciples and put them further and further away from the disciplines. If one can find a guru who will show techniques, then one is fortunate indeed.

If one follows a popularity-crazed guru, one cannot become liberated. It is impossible since the guru will be so caught up with numerous complications thrown before him by destiny that he will not be interested in one's advancement. Therefore if one is serious, one has to find a guru who is free from popularity.

One must also know how to get along with fellow disciples for if one tangles with them, one's spiritual progress may be checked. One must learn to remain in a low-key, humble position and stay clear of political complications. And as soon as one can, one must leave the forefield of the spiritual society and take a back seat. Then secretly but progressively one should tend to advancement. If one remains prominent politically, one will invariably be confronted with challenges of destiny that will cause bafflement leading to a callous disregard for self development.

Chapter 14

Methods of Attraction

Charm

Regardless of the spiritual techniques, the religion propagated and the character of the spiritual master, there are essentially four ways through which spiritual masters function:

- *charm*
- *theoretical knowledge*
- *spiritual experience*
- *techniques through which spiritual experience is gained*

Most of the spiritual masters in the modern era work through charm. Charm means that the spiritual master has a certain type of body, certain facial features, a certain way about him that attracts others, regardless of whether he does them any good or not. Most of the modern gurus work through charm. By this, people are easily made into disciples

Theoretical knowledge

Some spiritual masters work by giving lectures and writing books in which theoretical approaches to spiritual life are revealed. Regardless of whether the theory can be applied practically or not, these spiritual masters attract intellectuals.

As far as material existence is concerned, no one can be freed by theoretical knowledge. It is impossible but one can develop a sense of security by theoretical knowledge. That is possible. If the theoretical approach was adopted from a process that yielded success, it can give results if it is converted to practice. Otherwise the theory is useless and only serves to give mental satisfaction, without producing elevation.

Spiritual experience

A spiritual master who attracts disciples by description of spiritual experience may or may not be honest with the disciples. If he is honest, he will explain to them the disciplines through which he got the experiences.

Technique

Strictly speaking one can become liberated only by application of specific techniques which free one from the various modes of material nature. Otherwise liberation is impossible. Both the proficient spiritual master and the disciple must apply themselves for the liberation of the disciple. The spiritual master alone cannot achieve it. The disciple alone cannot either. Both have their portions of energy to contribute. If they cooperate with the process, the disciple will gradually and definitely shed illusion and be liberated

Chapter 15

Spiritual Master

without Disciples

One should not take a position as spiritual master so long as one's spiritual master uses a material body and is in good standing. If the spiritual master, however, is fallen, one may with caution become a spiritual master, but even then, to do so is risky, for those who suspect a spiritual master to be a fraud, are also suspicious of his disciples.

My own case will explain this. I had the inclination to join a religious society in 1973 but Providence did not permit me. Later on in 1978, when I did formally join that spiritual group, the founder passed on from this physical side of life. Subsequently, I had to take initiation from one of his disciples. It so happened that by a movement of providence, this Swami was disgraced.

In anyone questions me of my affiliation with that Society, I am afraid to answer. If I mention the name of that Swami, they say, "0, your guru was a fraud". If, however, I mention the name of the Society's founder, people say, "So many of his disciples are questionable." Thus I am defenseless. The point is: No one trusts a disciple of a fallen spiritual master, or a disciple of a spiritual master whose followers are reputed exploiters. This, however, can be converted into an asset if it makes the disciple bow his head and remain hidden and humble. False pride can hardly afflict such a person.

If one's spiritual master is fallen, certain energies might still abound which would prevent the safe assumption of guruship. Therefore one should be cautious. We must understand that mystic energy or supernatural power can affect our lives. Therefore we should not be eager to take a position as a guru. And besides, there is neither urgency nor necessity to take an official position.

Even without the pomp, honor and fame, one can instruct others effectively in spiritual life. I did this not only in this life but in previous lives as well. In fact, a person without official status may do more to free others. The unofficial spiritual helper is not restricted by the rules of institutions or by the rival gurus who compete for fame.

An official guru has many restrictions placed on him by disciples, by the government and by the public. In some cases, he is forced to speak untruthfully and to act against his interest. But an authority without official status has more initiative and originality. Formerly the celibate monks hardly functioned as official gurus. It was the householder ascetics who did it. Persons like Vasisht Rishi who acted as official gurus were householder ascetics. And there are many others like Vyasa, the author of the *Mahabharata*. Nowadays, many official gurus are celibate monks. I observed that people prefer a guru who is a single monk. This is due to a twofold pressure:

- **distrust of the public**
- **suspicion of sex desire.**

The public is distrustful of the sexual nature of a householder. Unless he lives apart from his wife, they are reluctant to treat him respectfully as a sinless, pleasure-resistant personality.

To sidestep these biases, one needs to get rid of the desire for pomp and formal recognition and be willing to help any person who is humble enough, plain and simple enough, to take spiritual assistance from wherever and from whomever he or she may get it.

Dr. Ramananda Prasad of the International Gītā Society had some suggestions concerning a book of this nature. Considering the recent upsurge of scandals and disgraces in many of the spiritual societies, his ideas are worth mentioning. He felt that these issues should be considered by those who are in responsible positions in spiritual societies as well as those mature individuals who are not attached to any of the established institutions. He felt that books of this nature should address the following issues:

- *How to avoid being enslaved by a guru.*
- *How to resist the ideas of gurus who say that you should surrender everything, your body, mind, and money to get liberation or salvation.*
- *How to avoid being trapped in a spiritual society or institution.*
- *Understanding the dos and don'ts of being a guru or being a disciple.*
- *How to prevent fall-down for the guru.*
- *How we can better serve the spiritual needs of seekers without forming a guru cult.*
- *Knowing some characteristics to look for in false gurus, and conversely in the genuine, fail-safe spiritual master.*
- *How to search for a guru in India and in the West.*
- *How to test for a genuine guru.*

I studied this list of concerns. It is a carefully thought-out list and could be the subject matter of a very important book. Each person who treks the path of spiritual life should be concerned and should note this listing. Each of us needs to know the answer to these questions. Even if we cannot match the ideal, knowing of it, would be valuable in putting us on the course of attaining that perfect situation.

In a sense, every guru is a disciple of someone and every disciple is a guru or at least an instructor of someone. Thus each of us needs to understand what Dr. Ramananda calls the dos and don'ts of being a guru and of being a disciple.

Some Astral Communications

On April 1 of 1996, Swami Satyananda of the Bihar School of Yoga came to me early in the morning to hand me a small book called the *Laughing Swami*. This was on the astral level. Later I got that book physically. It was published by Motilal in India, being written by Harry Aveling. Swami Satyananda used an astral body, like so many departed gurus and ascetics who were transferred out of the physical world after being displaced from material forms.

Handing me the book he said, "Read this. Give your assessment. In the final analysis, the householder ashram is the best. Developing the spirituality of oneself and a wife is the best. It always was so. The sannyasa position is one-sided. Please record this."

I replied, "I am sorry but I will not write this. I am not responsible for this statement."

He replied, "I said it. It is my consequence."

I argued for not writing it down. I said, "If I write it, a part of the consequence will come to me. I can only say it if I explain it fully. Otherwise I will add to the confusion."

But he persisted, "Write it down. We should work together. Those who are dead must take help from the living." Then he departed.

Later on that day he returned. He said, "I made a mistake. I sacrificed my development into my sense of compassion. I offered my progress to assist others. Then my development was curtailed. I heard that Vishnudevananda advised you against it. He did you a tremendous favor."

This remark was made about an instruction I received from an associate of Swami Satyananda. That person was Swami Vishnudevananda. Both of them were disciples of Swami Shivananda of Divine Life Society.

Sometime ago, Swami Vishnudevananda lay down a condition under which he agreed to instruct me in a course of hatha yoga. This was an astral course which I took from the Swami at night while my physical body rested. He said, "Do not help others at the expense of your development. Assist others as a side feature only. Helping others should not be the priority."

Thus I intend to be a spiritual master without disciples.

Chapter 16

Becoming a Guru

Before publication, when part of this book was reviewed, some persons were depressed by the information. One celibate monk read the book and remained silent about it. After being questioned, he said, "I do not like it. It is another guru-bashing book. There are enough of these. I prefer something that is in glorification of gurus." Needless to say, this monk is himself an official guru. He did not want his disciples to read a book which shows the flaws of spiritual masters.

Another sannyasi wrote that this was dangerous, having too much criticism that could be misused by Christian deprogrammers who are trying to destroy Eastern religious movements which are established in the West.

I have a question for all readers who desire to become guru:

What do you have to offer
which other gurus do not provide?

`Please think of it!`

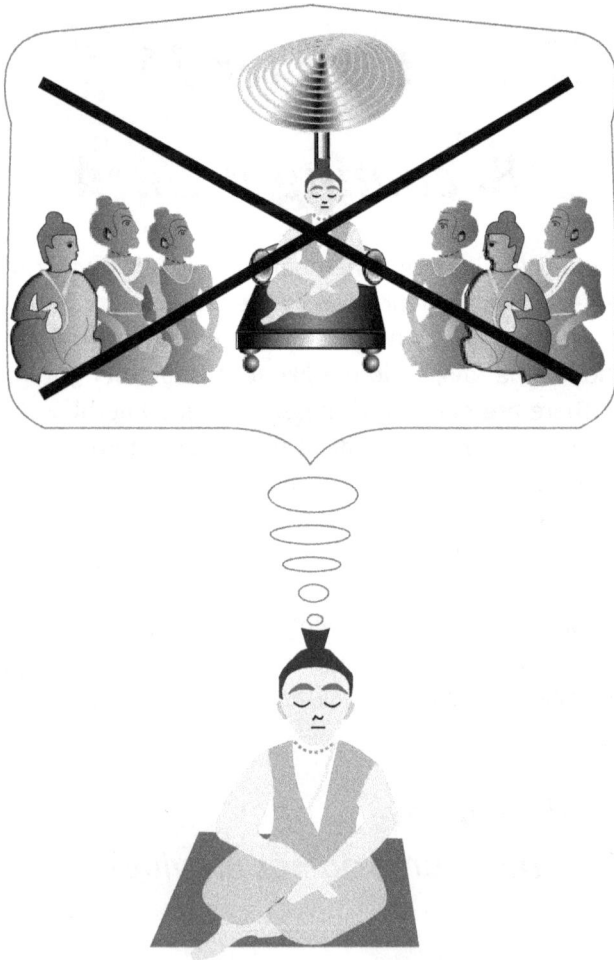

If you are going to offer something different, then I suggest that you reconsider. It would be better that you join with an established guru and assist him. Just search around in the East or West and find a guru that suits your liking. Find a guru who offers a salvation that is similar to the one you conceived. Assist him. Why start another society and increase the fragmentation of the spiritual effort?

There is another reason for you to join an established guru. Suppose you do become a guru. Since you are new at the role, you will make mistakes. After all, to err is human. But if you join a guru, you can see his mistakes and learn without being in the limelight directly. In this way, if perchance you do become a guru, you would have learned of the pitfalls of guruship. Take my advice. Will you?

If you have something different to offer, something that no guru is currently giving, then I still suggest that you hold off for a bit. Try to get scriptures. Read about the ancient gurus. See if you can find a guru of the past who had the same desires as you do. Study his biography. Consider it. Meditate deeply and try to reach him. After all, if someone already did what you plan to do, then that someone is existing somewhere. You may consult him. Get some inspiration from him. Now if you cannot contact him, then my friend, I still question your right to be a guru. Perhaps you do not qualify. Perhaps you should be realistic and scrap the plan.

If a street is lined with shopkeepers, why open another business? It is better that you do not. It would be better to develop your perfection quietly. Why get involved in a dangerous business like guruship?

If someone follows you wanting you to be his guru, ask him one question: What do you get in my association that an established guru cannot give you?

There is a question: Do you think it is possible to be a spiritual master without disciples?

A guru told me that it was not possible. He said, "A king requires a kingdom. A spiritual master requires disciples. A family man requires children. There is no meaning to a spiritual master without disciples."

A very logical view, is it not? Yes, but I disagree. A king certainly requires a kingdom because he is incomplete unless he can order commoners to do his bidding. A family man does require a family because he needs that to satisfy his possessive feelings. But a spiritual master does not necessarily require disciples, because spiritual development is self-fulfilling. The development itself is so complete, that disciples are not a necessity.

Regardless of a following, a spiritual master of real importance can be an authority without disciples. If you feel that to be a spiritual master you must have disciples, you are suffering from a misconception. This is what I mean.

Responsibility

Disciples are a responsibility. Despite the flamboyant attitude of popular spiritual masters, disciples do mean added responsibility. Most spiritual masters are not liberated but go through a pretense of liberation. Some of them are near liberation or were near to liberation at the time of their last intense austerities, but they desisted and returned to human society to capture disciples. For some of these former ascetics, their last intense austerity which brought them to a brink of perfection was in a past life, but they were diverted to establish an institution for disciples. Do you want to be forestalled in the same way? Do you want to live a life of pretentious ideas, giving a false sense of confidence to followers, promising but never delivering the salvation you advocate?

Do you actually think that you can liberate one single limited spirit? Do you feel that you can deliver even yourself?

Previously, a friend wrote complaining about another friend who functions as a guru. He said, "I do not know why he became a guru. It is madness. You and I know well that he does not qualify for this. Why did he take this guru position? It is his ruination. He is a pretense guru. He has not freed himself. How then can he free others or be their guru? His ambition is ridiculous. He has not seen the heaven of our God. How can he take others to an unseen, unproven, divine place?"

Chapter 17

The Envy Element

The envy element is one good reason not to become a guru. Instead of taking disciples, you may avoid this envy element by striving for perfection without taking disciples and by helping others without receiving honor, worship, or adoration.

The most essential basis for attraction between disciples and their spiritual master is the envy element. But this envy element, which is in a sense the destruction of the guru, is usually hidden under the disguise of the admiration element.

Since it is hidden most gurus do not see it for what it is. And so they become ruined by accepting disciples. To understand the envy element, we should study our psychology as human beings. The whole range of human relations is based on the envy principle, which is the principle of replacement. Material nature sponsors replacement.

The principle of envy and the principle of replacement works like this: A boy's grandfather was a postmaster. Seeing this the boy wanted to be a postmaster. He aspired and aspired, pressured and pressured his grandfather who was not interested in giving him the post. The elderly man worked his way up the ladder of government posts. Then he got that post mastership. He did not like the idea of resigning the post to his grandson. Still the boy knew that by the replacement principle, there was a much greater probability of the grandfather dying before him. Thus he waited and waited. When the grandfather passed on, the youngster got the position. No one contested his application. They assumed that since the grandfather had the position, the grandson was worthy of it. In this way, the grandson satisfied his envy through the principle of replacement. Since all these material bodies must die and since usually they die in old age, any youngster can depend on the principle of replacement.

Sometimes the principle of replacement does not operate to satisfy someone. Sometimes, suddenly and unexpectedly, it satisfies a person who was not fit for a position.

Listen to a story: There was a guru who came from India, a very flashy and lovable man. He got many disciples in the Western countries but as it is with the recurring principle of replacement, he died. This guru knew that he would die. In anticipation, he trained some men to replace him. He wanted his mission to continue after death. He was a very shrewd Indian. In any case it worked out that some of the trained disciples took leadership positions after he died. They pretended not to envy him but as I explained, the principle of envy is there as a constant factor in the shuffle of the material world.

I once served one of these replacement men. While I served him, the temptation to envy and then replace him, surfaced in me. I began to think, "He replaced the original man. Likewise, I could replace him. He assumed the glamour, fame and pomp of his predecessor. I could display the same things. When he is dead, I will take the leadership." In this way, I became crazier and crazier by the moment. Eventually however, I saw that the whole scheme was ridiculous. First of all the original man who came from India was not original. He took ideas from other religious leaders in India. He came to the West and established himself independently. Secondly, his disciple whom I envied was later disgraced. The glamour, fame and pomp destroyed him.

Since envy will be there in the material world, my suggestion is this: If you envy someone, check to see if you envy the correct quality in the person. Do not waste the envy. It is a very valuable energy that may propel you into the realm of salvation. Do not envy the flimflam, the glamour, the popularity and all such harmful things. For spiritual life, envy the austerity performed. Ask this: What was the austerity through which the guru became popular?

Do not bother with the popularity. Find the austerity. Even if the guru is not performing the austerity now, he performed it in the past. Find out about it. Envy that accomplishment. Besides that, a popular leader has nothing to offer to you. You are not going to improve unless you practice the appropriate austerities.

Envy, which is a very subtle motivating force, functions by the pleasure of dissatisfaction. But this dissatisfaction is an impulse that alerts us that we are not sitting in the position we are comfortable with. And to get the desired part, we should take up austerities. Even if our idea of the position is incorrect, still we will not understand the error if we do not take up austerities and by that acquired power, try to live out the idea.

When I had that idea to replace the man who replaced the guru from India, I studied the austerities of the man I wanted to replace. Gradually I learned these disciplines. I understood how he developed the power but I also saw that as one develops such power, one's personality becomes more and more distorted. I did not like the distortion. This is why I stopped those disciplines. It was a system through which one gets an attractive body, has beauty externally and remains functionally exploitive in character. Thus the austerity of a leader is the actual feature of envy, not the popularity.

A scaled-down model

There is yet another way to deal with envy and to get benefits from it in spiritual life. This is the method of small-scaling. In this method, one carefully studies the ways and means of the person being envied. Then one sets out to do exactly what he did on a small scale. If one is successful, one may expand further. But if one does not succeed or if one experiences the flaws of the predecessor, one may abandon the envy by realizing that the outcome is undesirable.

For instance, there are many householder ascetics like this writer. Some of us want to be gurus. That is our main ambition. Since, however, we are householders our aim is frustrated for the time being. We have this silly idea that unless we renounce our families, we cannot be gurus. This is a fool's view.

If we apply the principles of small-scaling, we can instantly be gurus by being authoritative in our families. Now suppose we try to be gurus over our families and we fail, then we can understand that we lack the force of authority. As some spiritual masters fumble around with disciples whom they cannot control, so a householder may awkwardly try to regulate his family. It is the same exhibition of struggling to control.

Do you really want to be a guru? Do you have a spouse? Do you have a child or two? Then be a guru by exercising control over those people. It is that simple. Try to be a guru on that small scale.

As a guru forms an institution which he desires to be perpetuated beyond death, so your family may be perpetuated after your body dies. What is the difference?

The guru leaves behind loyal disciples, who then mount his seat, take his honor and prestige. Your spouse or children may claim your assets after your death. What is the difference?

Chapter 18
The Transfer of Faith

The most powerful weapon of material nature in her fight against the gurus is the resistance to the transfer of faith. Let us analyze this. If you want to be a guru, you should consider that on this one aspect; material nature will fight you to the finish. As a guru, you challenge nature's influence over other entities. Nature will not allow you to liberate even one entity, without a struggle. And it will be a long and protracted fight, not a quickly-accomplished battle. Never mind those gurus who talk about instant liberation. Most of them are bluffers. They have no power to dictate instant release from material nature. Any ordinary spirit gets out after a long, tiresome struggle with his or her lower nature. The most a guru can do is to direct a disciple in how to fight lower tendencies.

The transfer of faith must occur in total before a guru can be successful with a disciple. In fact, the transfer of faith, if it is partial only, will cause the failure even of a capable guru. It does not matter if the guru is God in person. Even if he is God as in the case of Krishna, the guru of Arjuna, still until that transfer occurs, there is no success for the guru. It so happened that after showing Arjuna the Universal Form, Lord Krishna achieved success with Arjuna. He caused Arjuna to transfer the faith Arjuna had in material nature. But it is not so easy for other gurus, even if they claim to be working for Krishna. Most gurus do not have and will not have even a fraction of the power that Krishna exhibited to Arjuna.

Each person expresses faith in a particular process, often to such an extent that a superior method is shunned and avoided by that person. A man does not feel satisfied until he can express confidence in a customary way. Here is an example. In India there are various ways of doing a worship ceremony. But if we take a man from one part of India and send him to another area where the ritual is different, he may, by his training of tolerance, attend the ceremony but he will not have as much faith in it as he does in his native procedure. Even though the other type of ceremony may be superior, still the man will not feel satisfied until he can perform a traditional ritual. This means that he is unable to transfer his confidence to another tradition. He just cannot extract his faith from the familiar one.

In being a guru, and in trying to get disciples to follow a particular method, one has to fight contrary tendencies of the disciples. This struggle could last for years. Which of us desires to be such a fighting guru who fights, and fights and still does not get the full faith of the disciples?

Even if a disciple has faith in the guru, even if the method of the guru is traditional, still the disciple might only have faith in a particular allowance offered by the guru. He might not have confidence in the total discipline introduced.

In the case of a father, his children might have confidence in his allowances of money, clothing, food, and status, but they may have no confidence in his disciplinary management. And the father might fumble for years trying to transfer their faith from the conveniences to the disciplined life. Most fathers fail. And so do most gurus.

A guru can only liberate those entities who have faith in him. He can only do so if he has specialized techniques. General religious principles cannot free anyone because the bondage to material nature is intertwining and complicated. Even in cases where general principles are effective, there will be particular resistances which might not be removed by the guru and which would remain to thwart his influence.

In a battle, many soldiers of a battalion may seem to be gung-ho and loyal to their country, but there are little resentments and other resistant aspects in the nature of each soldier. A disciple's confidence in a guru is a very good sign of the success of the guru but it is not the whole truth.

Material nature works steadily to undermine the efforts of the guru. The individual nature of each entity tries to buff itself against the leader in many minute but disruptive ways which serve to cancel out the efforts of the guru.

Generally speaking, religion does not treat men and women equally. Usually certain aspects facilitate men and others facilitate women, as the case may be. Each gender should test the religion in specific ways. Generally speaking, religious leaders specialize in assisting one sex or the other.

If you want to be a spiritual master you may have to consider which gender you desire to assist the most. Are you going to free men or women? Or do you think that you can free either? When it gets right down to practice, you should specialize in one or the other, all depending on your nature and ability to attract one sex or the other. Regardless of what your religion says, your personality may attract one more than the other. It is not your religion but your personality which dictates the attraction of one sex or the other.

Let me cite an experience. Some years ago, I had this idea that I could be a spiritual master. I was very eager and enthusiastic. Even though I accepted a spiritual master, he was unknown and had no institution. I attracted some disciples, mostly on the basis of serving as their religious leader in a past life. At the time, I had a natural power. I did not need institutional support, or credentials from an established lineage. My subtle body was ready for it urged me on and on, on the basis of my role as a guru in a past life. At the time I was not married. My youthful body had no sexual experience. I felt that women were neutral. I did not note gender influences. This was a naive view of human relations, an underestimation of sex interaction.

I began to teach. I opened up a small teaching place. Providence encouraged me by sending disciples from a past life. As it turned out, this was a big joke that providence was to play on me. Even though they were disciples from a past life and even though they recognized that I was their guru from the past, they still could not place their confidence fully. They had acquired confidence in the new ethnicity and in the new society their bodies grew in. I could not shift that confidence. Thus I failed as an authority.

Some disciples were females, but while in the past life, they were married and had sexually reformed bodies, in this new life, they were single, lusty, and bold. They made sexual demands. I was not prepared for this. It became an awkward situation in dealing with those females and their sexual needs.

Seeing that I was just about to make a fool of myself, providence decided to call off the joke and ease me by making difficult complexities which caused many females to go away. But still I was intimately confronted by a few females. So this is the situation. One must, if he is to be a guru, consider the sexual aspect. Unless you live in a morally-restrictive society, the acceptance of women disciples, especially single women, will jeopardize your morality. Avoid it completely. We should treat the path of leadership with great caution, adjusting ourselves as we proceed. We should not dare to assume that because we have confidence, nothing will go wrong.

Women disciples

If you want to make women disciples, you should consider these factors: First their social needs must be considered. Let us suppose that a young lady wants to become my disciple. I should know her status as being married or single. If she is not married, what are her plans for matrimony? If she is married, what will my relationship be with her husband? If he will not be my disciple, then whose disciple will he be? How will my teachings to his wife affect their relationship?

Will there be a conflict between the mode of behavior I request of the married lady and the one her husband desires? How will this conflict be resolved? If I do not think over these aspects carefully, it would be my whim only to make such a lady a disciple. But many religious leaders do exactly that. They carelessly create social complications.

In the case of the unmarried lady, what are her prospects for marriage? Will she marry to one of my disciples? Should I suggest that she marry a man who is under my influence? Suppose she does marry one of my male disciples; what should I do if they prove to be incompatible? Many famous teachers marry two disciples, and then the married couple separates. What are my chances of succeeding when so many teachers failed?

If a female disciple is married, her sexual needs will be fulfilled by her husband, not by me. Thus I will not have to deal with that part of her life. But what of those who do not marry; what is their status? What happens to their sexual urges? I know of some former single monks, who started preaching missions and who became sexually involved with one or more of their unmarried female disciples. What was their intention?

It would mean, therefore, that to be a spiritual master and to have young women disciples, might be impractical unless I functioned in a morally restrictive society. Even in the case of elderly spiritual masters, this support from a moral environment is required. I have seen an elderly spiritual master become distracted by young women who rendered personal service. He became so distracted that even though he was a senior monk with vows not to be involved with women, he used to allow young women to wash his underwear and to cook for him. He got involved in their weddings, conducting ceremonies for them, and seeing that their social needs were fulfilled. He went so far as to arrange some marriages to his male disciples. Just as a father may get involved in the adult stages of his daughter's body, so some of these elderly spiritual masters literally follow their female disciples into bridal chambers to be sure that the ladies are treated with traditional regard.

Since these girls may do worship services for these spiritual masters, or render services that pertain to worship services, some elderly gurus inquire about the status of their menstrual cycle, since ceremonial rules prohibit women to do ritual worship during the menstrual period. All of this must be considered if you want to be a spiritual master.

Sexual needs of male disciples

Even with men, there are sexual problems. If, for instance, you become a spiritual master and your body is lustily inclined, you will definitely have trouble with attraction either to women, men or both genders. Some missionaries believe that since services rendered to a preaching mission or to a temple are rendered for God, such services cannot have a lusty impact. But in this respect, they are wrong. Religion or no religion, if there is interaction and services rendered, there will be exchange of sexual energies.

Even with men, there are sexual problems. Recently some spiritual masters who came from India to the Western countries attracted many homosexuals and even though they did not have gross sexual relationships with the men, the energy flowed around them and affected their missions. In some cases, it ruined their missions, as some homosexuals who got high positions breached celibate vows.

Putting aside the homosexuals, what about male disciples who have no homosexual orientation. Can any of these imperil a spiritual master?

Let me cite a few cases. One young man who had a heterosexual sexual orientation, got attracted to a female disciple of his spiritual master. At first this young man wanted to be a monk. His guru who was enthusiastic and confident gave the monk status to the young man. A few years later, it was discovered that a female disciple of the guru had made sexual contact with the youngster. The girl was pregnant. The guru then got involved and married the young man. Let us look at this. First the guru was naive enough to think that the young man could be a celibate monk. Secondly the guru covered and rationalized the sexual contact the youngster had with the female disciple. Then the guru got them married. This is called an implication. In that case, the guru functioned more as the father of the youngster.

With the marriage completed, the guru kept a close eye on the couple. All went well for a time. There was a child. The couple proved useful to the guru for a few years and then it was found that the youngster made a sexual relationship with another young woman. His wife was frustrated. She went to the guru and complained, "My dear Guruji, my husband, your disciple, had a sexual contact with another of your female disciples. What should I do? He is now staying with that woman, most of the time. I do not see him often. He does not treat me well." After this the guru called the young man and lectured extensively, but still the young man could not break away from his new girlfriend. The new female was irresistible.

In another case, a skilled young man became near and dear to his authority. Some female disciples of the guru wanted to marry that young man but he resisted and resisted, claiming that marriage was not for him. He said, "I am not interested in women; I want to be useful to my guru. If I get married, I will have to decrease the service. I will never marry."

Considering the good example, the guru took pride in this young man. The guru appreciated the young man's resistance and loyalty. Still, young girls offered to be the wife of the young man and still he resisted. In the meanwhile, his body had reached sexual maturity. Since he had no celibate practice of austerity, his body became lusty. Since he was so near and dear to his guru, he ate gourmet foods just like his authority. These foods increased his lusty nature but neither he nor his guru could realize this. They believed that their foods were holy and could only give a holy effect.

Then the youngster used to have dreams with young ladies. These were dreams of a sexual nature. Sometimes a young lady whom he saw during the day would be kissing him in dreams during the night. Sometimes another lady would be undressing.

Sometimes he would find himself in sexual contact in dreams even though he never had sexual relations physically.

Gradually he was forced into the habit of masturbation to relieve himself. Thus having male disciples could be a problem for a spiritual master. How should a spiritual master regulate the sexual nature of a male or female disciple? Should he act haphazardly? Should he pose as a know-it-all and still be very naive in actuality?

By now the readers might get my point: I discourage assumption of the spiritual master status. Why? The reason is this: You can develop spiritually and make progress without taking the formal position as spiritual master. You can assist others without being their formal religious leader. It can be done. Thus why should you risk yourself, a set of disciples, and the spiritual quest, by becoming a spiritual master haphazardly?

If even with male disciples you will have to manage sexual needs, then is it worth it to be a spiritual master? Are you qualified to manage complex sexual energies?

Chapter 19

Being Attracted

to Guru Importance

Without a certain spiritual teacher, a person's spiritual life might be nil. I know of cases of persons who would not have had any spiritual interest, if they had not spoken to specific gurus. But this does not mean that the guru must have an official position. A guru, if he is that important to you, does not require an official position. You can function as a guru to others without having an official position. The importance of a guru is not his adoption of officialness but rather his ability to deliver someone from the perils of material existence. And he can do that even if he is not in an official capacity. Thus if I or you desire to assist others or if I or you have spiritual importance in the life of another, then we do not have to be officials. We do not need the support of a position or an institution.

There are spiritual masters, however, who convey the idea that the official position is absolutely necessary for functionality. They portray themselves as being men of position, as if to explain that without their positions, they would have no effectiveness in human society. If we are lured by this sort of guru, then we may, in imitation, also become men of position. But still, this sort of role is not essential to the development of disciples, at least not to deep-seated development. It might contribute to a superficial relationship between a spiritual master and a disciple but no matter how flamboyant that relationship is, it still is superficial. This is why we see that after years of such flamboyant treatment, some disciples turn sour and speak against the guru. Some go as far as to itemize his deviations.

Even though one may be attracted to a guru because of his flamboyance and style, this is not really why anyone is attracted to a guru. The essential reason is **personal relationship**.

Without the personal relationship, no one stays with a guru no matter how official he is. One may be attracted to a guru by something luxurious, but one does not remain at his feet if he takes no personal interest at some time or the other. All who come, wait for a day, week, month or year for one special thing; a relationship with the guru and a personal, direct relationship, too. But that connection can develop without formality and pomp. One does not have to lick the toes of some other person just to acquire their care and concern. Thus any of us can function as a spiritual advisor without having others kiss the dust of our feet. We can be important in the lives of others without having them sing our praises, chant our name daily and adore us as we sit adorned in the best silken clothes on embroidered high seats. It is possible.

A guru might well be indispensible in the life of one disciple, but he may not be that essential in the life of another. In some spiritual societies, a spiritual teacher inspires his favorite disciples to spread the word around, that he is indispensible to all disciples and to humanity as well. Whether this is just a preaching tactic or whether these gurus actually believe this, is another matter.

I can tell you this much: If you are indispensible to a disciple, you do not need to be in an official position to administer the saving grace to him. It can be done without the pomp and ceremony. And why force or induce others to treat you with that sort of respect?

If you can assist someone a little but you are not indispensible to their spiritual life, why not do it in a quiet way, humbly? Why force the person to come before you as a disciple? Why be that ugly about the matter? Can you not help someone without officialness and recognition? Are you that hungry for honor? Why allow your favorite disciples to form a fence around you, through which no one can reach you, even for the smallest favor you might render?

Chapter 20

Impure Gurus/Fallen Gurus

It is said that an impure or fallen guru was never a guru since the term guru implies a grave, divine being. But such a statement is a theoretical proposal only. In this mundane creation, there is nothing that is perfect to an errorless degree. The idea that a guru cannot be fallen at any time is fool's idea only.

Human beings should be content with the fallen gurus or impure gurus. To think that we must have pure or non-fallen spiritual leaders is to put ourselves on a very high pedestal and to situate ourselves in a mood of false pride. Are we worthy of a perfect guru? The truth is: We are not.

What we really need in a guru is honesty and continued progression away from impurities and away from fallen conditions. We need him to set an example of how to shed vices and various contaminations. Only those who think that they can be miraculously saved without their own endeavor, feel that they need a perfect guru. In fact, an imperfect guru is more useful than a perfect one if that imperfect authority marches out of the filth and spiritual uncleanliness that surrounds us.

Those who work up a steam about salvation are mostly compassionate but exploitive preachers who are simply fooling us with empty promises. They are expert at absorbing our religious confidence, expert at encouraging us to be complacent, expert at flashing before us useless, worthless, hopeless, scrappy but good-sounding means of salvation.

Unless we are willing to work our way out of this materialism, no one, not even God can help us, because we will remain embedded in the association of material nature, under its bewitchment. Our emotions work against us so what can God do if we do not realize ourselves, and take assistance from Him for self-reform? Up to this point, God, for all He is, has not dislodged us from the romance with material nature. But all of a sudden a preacher takes a platform to tell us that we will be saved. Well, we are not ready. God is there but under the present circumstances material nature is much closer. We are more attached to her than we are to an unseen, non-manifest God.

Perfect gurus are unnecessary and imperfect ones who are stagnant or who are retrogressing, require our sympathy. What we need is an imperfect guru who strives, and through that striving can show us effective ways of keeping the filth of material existence from clinging to us. Such imperfect gurus who are presently aspiring, who are ahead of us in the race for perfection, who act as an encouragement and inspiration, are required.

An impure guru, even if he strives, cannot free me. That I admit, but what I want is a process of freedom that works progressively, not just a description of a scriptural promise. What is the use of an idealized religion and guru which effectively gives no salvation?

Becoming a guru

In this book, I make a deliberate effort to discourage you, from becoming a guru. Those of you who are gurus already should heed warnings. Those of you who are determined to be gurus, should take advice.

Fulfill your guru desires but do so cautiously. Do not become over confident. First you need a friend who does not care about your honor and pomp, your showmanship and grand actions. You need a detached friend. Find such a friend. Keep him near you. Ask his opinion regularly. I was such a friend to a guru but he did not like my non-patronizing opinions. Once he invited me to a confidential meeting. When I arrived there, I listened. I was appalled at what was discussed. I said to myself, "What is this, a spiritual society or a ring of hoodlums?"

Later on I saw my friend, the guru, and I questioned him. I said, "You asked me to attend the meetings. I did so. What is my position? Should I remain quiet or should I give a view?"

He replied, "Always give your view, especially if you hear something that you do not like, something that disturbs you."

I thought, "O yes! He is balanced and broad-minded. He will listen to another's view."

At the next meeting when I spoke, my friend became angry. In the middle of the meeting, he burst out, "You should not say this to me. I am the leader. You have to respect me. You should not give a counter-view."

So that is it. My advice is that you should not be that sort of guru. You should have one friend who is detached and who can fearlessly tell you it like it is. It is said that Rama of the *Ramayana* fame, asked some friends to speak of the public opinion. When they informed him, he received unfavorable news. People gossiped about the recovery of his wife after she was kidnapped and kept prisoner by a foreign ruler. Rama heard this. He acted on it. He did not reject his friends. If we are going to be gurus anyway, let us follow his example in hearing the frank opinion of friends.

I have another piece of advice. What is your spiritual discipline? Will you continue it, even if you have disciples? Or will you become so occupied managing followers that you will have no time for practice?

Established gurus

For those of you who are established gurus with many followers or who intend to be recognized, I do have some advice. As Dr. Prasad requested, one should understand the dos and don'ts of being a guru and even of being a disciple. If you do not understand this and you become a guru, you will learn by trial and error. And that would be a sham.

Established gurus have insurmountable problems. Those who are supported by a time-tested tradition, usually survive the guruship. The revolutionaries who either reject a good tradition or undermine it, for one reason or the other, usually fail at the bid. There are many reasons for the fall of an established authority.

I attribute it to one cause: the monopolization of power. This exploitation is a complex issue. It has to do with a strong desire for putting one's mark on history. You may have heard of the great conquerors such as Ravan, Alexander the Great, Genghis Khan, and Caesar. In modern history, you may have heard of rulers like Napoleon, Adolf Hitler, Mao Tse Tung and others. But their singular problem was the monopolization of consolidated power. Even if you inherit political or religious power, still you cannot consolidate it and maintain it, if you do not have the intelligence to manage an organization. Successful rulers and spiritual teachers who inherited power, must be given credit for their ability to consolidate and use the authority. But how many of them were able to distribute the power?

Keeping power to oneself is easy. A higher, more complex aspect is the distribution of power. Nature does not like a leader who keeps all power. Nature works for the collapse of his empire. If a leader systematically distributes power, he can rule for a long time. And after he leaves his body, his influence positively persists.

Efficient distribution of consolidated power is not easy. Many people talk about it and criticize those rulers and religious leaders who failed to accomplish it. But it is a difficult accomplishment for anyone. Before you can distribute power, you should find qualified disciples to bear the allotted energies. If you cannot find such people, you may have to train novices in the art. That takes time and energy.

Once you consolidate power, your next step will be to maintain it. Power is like money. Power does not like to stay with a man who cannot maintain it. Thus the first step, consolidation, must be supported by the knowledge of power maintenance. It may be said, however, that power is to politics as kind concern is to religion. However, in this case, we are just shuffling words. Religious influence is a form of politics; it is a very subtle form of it. Religion includes politics. Politics borders on the territory of religion.

Once an insignificant politician stated that he hoped to be a religious leader in his next life. He supported this desire with the argument that while he was a politician and had some control over a small territory, a friend of his, a priest controlled the hearts of people instead. The point is that politics has to do with the control of lands and human endeavor, while religion focuses on the control of human emotions and confidence. What is the difference? It is all management of various types of energy and of people who exploit such energies. Politics is mostly physical with some mystical reach. Religion is mostly mystic with physical reach.

Once you consolidate the power, the next step is to maintain it. Once you learn how to maintain it, the next step is to find disciples who can help you share the weight of it. Power has weight. In fact, mystic power, psychic or spiritual power, has even more weight than political power. As we all know, in the material world, the more physical or gross an object is, the heavier it is. Compare a feather to a nail. Compare a cloud to a bucket of water. Nature easily floats a cloud but it may take her weeks to lift a bucket of water by gradual evaporation.

When we look in the direction of the physical, that law has application, but when we look in the direction of the spiritual, those laws are reversed. In the spiritual direction, the closer we get to the spiritual, the lighter the material side appears. Try to lift a feather with mental power without handling it in any other way. You cannot do it. Even though the feather is so light, you cannot move it. But if you try to lift up a bucket of water, something that will take weeks for nature to move, you can do it just by gripping the handle and carrying it off.

Training disciples to handle, consolidate, and maintain power is a very difficult task. I tried repeatedly. I became frustrated in my effort to train others to share whatever spiritual authority I consolidated. Just the other day, I decided to stop consolidating, stop maintaining, stop training others and just steady myself in spiritual life and forget all about establishing a spiritual society or institution. In other words, I cannot do it. It is beyond capacity.

One great man I know, established a spiritual society. He made claims about his missionary activities. He showed the world his trained followers. Later on, after he passed on, the society crumbled. Another great man I know, also established a spiritual society. He trained some men. But later, they left the society and he was forced to train others. There are some successes in such training but mostly, there are failures. Most of the gurus, even the ones in good standing, are bluffers. Study the history of their rise to power and you will see. Most of them make claims that neither they, their God nor institution can substantiate.

Some years ago, I stayed at an ashram. The guru did not live at the ashram but a leading disciple who was proficient at the technique, did. Once the guru sent an Indian gourmet cook. This cook came from India, especially to train some disciples in the fine art of Indian cooking. This Indian cook had a cooking skill. He could take anything and convert it into a delicious meal. I got to know him. Since he recently moved to America, he formed a close friendship with me because I could relate to him culturally.

Once he wanted to visit an Indian family in a nearby city. He had no car of his own. I possessed a small vehicle so I volunteered to take him. When we arrived at the Indian boutique shop, he introduced me.

As it was the rule at the ashram, I wore religious clothing. Seeing me in religious garb, the Indian lady we visited said, "O, you are an Indian." But before I could reply the cook said, "O yes, he is a greatly advanced yogi from India." He was joking as he always did but the lady thought it was true, I stood there dumbfounded with folded hands saying, "Pranam! Pranam!" which was the customary greeting.

They began talking in Hindi and Punjabi. I could not understand a word of it. However, the lady was still not satisfied. After a while, she returned to me, smiled, clasped her hands and said, "Please relax, sadhu. We are in the boutique business. You are in the religious business. We are not that different are we?" All I could say was "Pranam,"

The point the lady stressed was this: Most of the saintly attired monks (sadhus) are cons. Most of the spiritual masters are a rip off. They sell religion just the way she sold brass curios. Just as a merchant promises that his goods are the very best, even though they are of inferior grade, so many gurus promise that their religion is top notch, even though the system would not yield salvation.

On October 20 of 1996, I was paid a visit by a great yogi friend and teacher who gave me much information about the practice of pranayama and hatha yoga. He came to check on my practice. I was on the physical side. He, having lost his material body, was on the subtle side. He checked my routine and said, "Everything seems to be improving for you. You reduced social interest. You increased the disciplines. It does not matter what happens provided you maintain the practice. Forget the benefits of it. Just continue the practice. Many ancient ascetics got results from these austerities. Results will manifest gradually. Give no thought to it. Maintain the disciplines. Invest yourself in the practice."

After this he left.

So that is my position. I lost interest in consolidating, maintaining and distributing religious power. Fortunately, my teachers do not want me to become an official guru, they feel that I do not qualify. And it may be that they are jealously guarding me, thinking that if I take the high road to guruship, I will abandon their shelter. In any case, what do I have to lose? If they keep me as a student only, and do not want me to assume authority over others, then it is all for my gain. But you, what about you? You want to be a spiritual master? Okay! Take advice to avoid the pitfalls of guruship.

Once you get a few people trained, there will be problems. Some of those trained people will rebel. Some will walk away and leave you. Have you not heard? When Jesus Christ, the Lord that he is, was arrested for treason and for trying to establish his own church, some government officials asked a prominent disciple if he knew Jesus. The disciple denied. He said, "I do not know the man." He was asked on three occasions and consistently denied.

It is like that. Some followers will desert you. Consider one thing; there is a reason for the rejection of you. The reason is valid. Find the reason. Consider it. Let me relate an experience. I once trained a young lady in yoga techniques. This was in 1972 when I first began teaching to small groups. To tell you the truth, I really did not know what I was doing but I had an intuitive sense about it. Even though it was a tendency from a past life, I cannot honestly say that I was fully conscious of my activities. Much information from the past life was in the subconscious mind at the time. The lady took the training. She knew me from a past life. We understood each other quite well. After some time I asked her to teach others but she rejected the proposal. She said, "Go to hell, old man! I am not a teacher. Whatever I learnt from you, I will practice for myself. To hell with the world! I do not want people to regard me the way they relate to you as a wise old guff."

You could just imagine the shock. I trained her. I felt she was indebted but she rejected a commitment. I once trained a boy in Trinidad. This was in 1974. After he was trained and got some success, he made a promise to continue the practice and help me later on. His father objected and told him that if he practiced yoga any further, the funds for his education would stop. After that the boy dropped me as an instructor. It was a shock and a great loss because I invested much training in him. What his father meant was this: If he continued yoga, there would be no money for his education. The father would cease paying for it. Thus the boy had to choose a priority. This he did and our relationship ended then. I never heard from him again.

The point is: Some selected students will reject the teacher. But the teacher should not take it personally. For one thing: You are not God. You are subordinate to providence. Most of all: No matter how providence opposes you, always know this: Providence is the universal intelligence.

If you are going to be a guru or if you are already a guru, you should outmaneuver material nature by deliberately shattering your monopolization of any consolidated power. This applies mostly to exhibited power. Power which is not displayed, should be invested in your spiritual advancement to convert you into a spiritual master without disciples. But the power which you displayed can be safely handled only by sharing it. This sharing is a special time-consuming responsibility. Unless you share power with competent people, it will ruin you.

Unless one intends to share something one should not exhibit it. This is a law of nature. Thus if one develops a power and if one displays it, one will by the force of nature, have to share it. If in trying to share it one discovers that the beneficiaries cannot grasp it or acquire it, one has the added responsibility of preparing them to take it. For instance if a mechanic develops a more efficient engine, other mechanics who are familiar with an old style engine might not be able to service it. They require special training. Thus the burden of this new education is placed on the developer of the new motor. Since he invented the mechanism, he automatically becomes tagged for the responsibility of educating others about it. If on the other hand, he can keep his new engine out of sight, he may avoid that law of nature that stipulates sharing.

An ascetic is taught this lesson of sharing repeatedly. When he becomes disgusted with it, he stops displaying mystic powers to others. He develops himself secretly and poses in human society as a dotard, a fool, a non-ambitious person. There were many successful ascetics who posed as foolish men, as bums towards society and who were in fact, the most perfect, the most proficient of human beings. These personalities discovered efficient ways of perfection and still they hid themselves away under the garb of being useless human beings.

Some time in 1973, I visited Trinidad. I had yoga students there. We used to have lively discussions about reincarnation and spiritual life. We used to practice intense bhastrika pranayama in the tropical climate. Actually we did not know what we were doing, but in the fever of having youthful bodies we were doing this as a way of proving ourselves to society as youths usually do. Once I noticed a saintly man squatting on the pavement in Port-of-Spain, the capital city. I did not say anything to him, but I was happy for having seen the man. Just the look of the man brought to my mind, thoughts of spiritual freedom.

I got one of the youths who studied yoga with me. We went to Port-of-Spain. From the look of the man one could tell that he had not taken a bath in months. His meager body wrap and skin were dust gray. I inquired of the boy who was with me, "What do you think of him?"

He said, "He is a beggar. He does not bathe. He does not work. He hardly eats anything. He is useless. Let us go from here."

I said, "No, let us talk to him."

The boy came along because as youths we always liked anything curious or exciting, our main business was to discover something exciting. I squatted near the man. The boy did too. I said, "Can you give us some advice, sir. We are trying to get on a spiritual path. Any assistance you can render us will be of great service."

He waved his hand and said, "That is good. That is good. Keep on with your quest."

The boy was shocked. Hearing this reply, he moved closer to listen. I then said, "Sir, as you can see, we are young men. We practice yoga and get information about reincarnation. We feel that we used to exist before taking these bodies. What is your advice at this stage?"

The old Indian then changed his mood entirely. He said, "Just worship Jesus Christ. He is the God. There is no doubt about it. There were others, Krishna, Rama, and Mohammed. They are not ordinary. They are the God, believe me. I used to see Christ because I wanted to find out if he, too, was God because I am from a Hindu family. Once I saw Jesus in the sky. He was radiant, all light. He is one of these God people. Anyway, you boys have Christian parents. Worship Christ and everything will be alright for you. I cannot say anything else."

After this we went away. My friend was elated. Even though he was practicing yoga and reading Bhagavad Gītā, still he was attached to his Christian background. He was born in a devout Catholic family. I was not satisfied. But I was pleased to hear that the old man had gone that far as to check the divinity of Jesus Christ.

Later on I went back to the old man but he did not say anything. He was silent and did not reveal himself. I was like a customs officer who knows for sure that a certain traveler boarded an aircraft with a prohibited article, but after searching the traveler, the article was not found. Where did the article go?

Thus, like the old man, one should hide success in spiritual practice. Or one must be prepared to share with others and begin a system of educating others who are unfit for it. We must be responsible for whatever we display in human society. We must absorb the envy, resentments and resulting reactions which are produced by a display of expertise. For this reason many ascetics who were near to perfection, hide themselves from the public.

Let us consider what happens if one does not share the consolidated power or does not share the displayed perfection.

As soon as one takes a selfish stance with an energy or ability, one involves the envy of others. Some foolish spiritual masters, however, not being aware of the danger, enjoy such envy. But as soon as one begins to enjoy the resentment and envy of others, someone in one's association develops sympathy towards the opponents, and initiates a destructive force.

One who does not share the power but who displays it, will attract disciples who want power. These disciples, however, upon discovering that the teacher monopolizes, will play a service game with him in the hope of pleasing him so that he may transfer the ability. If he cannot or does not transfer it, strained feelings are felt between him and the followers.

Chapter 21

Appreciation

Appreciation affects both the spiritual master and his disciples. When a disciple feels that he is not appreciated, his services to the authority may be affected. But those who are consciously motivated in getting a particular thing from a guru, maintain their services even if they are not appreciated. Others become lax and fidgety as soon as they sense that the guru neglected them.

A spiritual master is apt to overlook services rendered by his disciples. It may not be a deliberate denial or a decision to ignore particular disciples; still the lack of appreciation is noticed by disciples who react in one way or another.

When a spiritual master gets much honor from disciples, he may take their services lightly and gradually they become alienated from him. Due to the focus on popularity, the guru hardly notices the services which are performed for him. And so, regrettably, he tramples on certain disciples. Some spiritual masters who become famous develop a visionary flaw through which they become blind to small services rendered by seemingly insignificant disciples. As a result, the society gradually but surely collapses.

If a spiritual master becomes famous worldwide, some disciples may hide their dissatisfaction. Still, this hiding has an effect, since their gripes and resentment surface in other areas to abort the mission of the guru. If he is indebted to them for services and does not appreciate or reward them appropriately, providence takes action to cut him down.

Some spiritual masters avoid being cut down before they leave their material bodies, while others are shredded before our very eyes. The ones who escape the shame, disgrace, and ridicule, do venture into the hereafter and face trouble in that subtle domain, or they are born again to face it in another life by new complications.

Some people who oppose a spiritual master in one life, were his chief or minor disciples in a past life. Since they passed off from a previous body with resentments towards him, they meet him again to settle the old grievances.

For instance, in this current life, I have met many persons who were my students in other lives. Some of them were out to get me. In a past life, I may have accepted service. I may have given a slogan for false salvation to someone. I may have cheated a man by taking money for missionary purposes and then squandered it away for personal maintenance. I may have lusted for someone's wife, but I may have done that under the pretension of causing the man's wife to come to a church, temple, or mosque. I may have encouraged a man in performing criminal acts to acquire money for my religious institution.

Such people may have met with hardships and embarrassments by my influence. Thus when I meet them in a new life, they are instinctively distrustful and resentful. A spiritual master who forgets to appreciate or who exploits, will suffer eventually,

In the present life, I compensate some obligations from past lives. But if I were a guru, it would be inconvenient to do so. The desire for fame would keep me distant from self interest. Since I avoid fame, I have ample chance to repay obligations, to ease old resentments and free myself from many complications.

There are cases, however, of spiritual masters who were disliked even by the individuals they assisted. It is like a medical case, where a doctor makes an accurate diagnosis, performs a successful surgery, but still the patient sues him for malpractice and wins the case. By twirls of destiny, I experience resentments from persons who were assisted fittingly by me in a past life and who again, in this life demand more services.

Some gurus set up a death trap for themselves by creating a barrier shield of favorite followers. These followers act as filters for the guru. In that situation, every new person who approaches, must work his or her way through a series of important disciples until at last the guru is directly confronted. This procedure which is a political screening process, does cause the downfall of some gurus. The screeners are usually condescending to newcomers. They harass new recruits, except that some of the new recruits may be saintly people who are worthy of their respect. By manhandling such saintly people, they bring ruination to the guru.

A hunger for power and a need for a dignified appearance, affects some gurus. As soon as they become famous they hide their ugly selves behind a screen of protocol. This protocol is a procedure of officialness. From behind such a screen, the guru projects an image of infallibility. He actually believes that every other human being is his subordinate. But eventually, he is ruined.

Some gurus create an official course for followers. This means that if one requires only one skill from a guru, one might have to pay the price of getting other skills even though they are unnecessary for one's spiritual development. This is a type of guru blackmail. I lived in many spiritual societies and associated with many gurus who perpetuated this nonsense. It works like this: You may require one skill. But the guru will insist that you learn something else and that you must serve for this other teaching. In some cases this stipulation is justified and in others it is not. If, for instance, I need to learn algebra, I will have to learn arithmetic first. If I want to study world history, a teacher might insist that I get a basic understanding of local history first. But when I wanted to learn Sanskrit, a teacher, told me to study Hindi even though that is not necessary.

In another example, when I began studying kundalini yoga at Yogi Bhajan's ashram in 1972, I was told that I had to work at their restaurant without wages. I washed huge pots under steam pressure at 11 pm at night. I had no desire to be a pot washer but it was part of the course. It had to be done if I lived at the ashram. In addition, I worked a full time job during the day and paid a rent for the little area I used on a dirt floor in a cold basement.

Yogi Bhajan did not live at the ashram. He lived some 800 or more miles away. I did not get along well with the leader of the ashram. This leader, the yogi's disciple, suspected that I was there for only one aspect of their practices which was to learn the techniques of bhastrika pranayama. In any case, Yogi Bhajan did come there once but he was not a flamboyant guru. He did not require anyone to bow to him as a mandatory procedure.

Some other gurus, however, are not like this. They establish a system of learning which forces all newcomers to go through a series of practices regardless of whether the practices are needed by the individual seekers or not. They charge either money, services or both for the practices. In some societies, services are stressed. These services are sometimes branded as seva or selfless-service, bhakti or devotional service, even though in some cases it is merely a personal service to a guru or to an agent of the guru. For the sake of money some gurus set up a system requiring that the disciple bring in a certain quantity of money daily or weekly. In one ashram, followers used to go out and do anything to get the money. The guru was only concerned to get the money and was not particularly interested in the means of acquiring it. This recklessness destroys the mission of the guru.

If you want to be a guru, you should consider. How will you avoid these pitfalls?

If I come to you to get one discipline, and I do not become your 100% follower, will you reject me or will you be willing to work with me on that one aspect, take services from me only for that and not try to squeeze me or have your disciples intimidate me because I do feel no need to become your full-time disciple?

Chapter 22

The Tricks of Disciples

As a guru you will have to deal with the tricks of disciples. These are actually the tricks of providence but they are played out consciously or unconsciously by disciples. A spiritual master, because of preoccupation with missionary ambitions, may or may not perceive these tricky factors.

If you become a guru and do not perceive these adjustments, you will be ruined either while living in the present body or after leaving the body and living in the hereafter or even when you return to this world through a baby form.

Certain disciples are salvation-hungry types. These are the most dangerous disciples. By nature, such disciples would believe anything a guru might tell them about how to earn salvation. They would even follow a method that is impractical. There are many human beings who would follow any religious leader who speaks convincingly about a method of salvation and who advocates a system that is based on the strength of the follower's belief. How will you protect yourself from such disciples?

Since, by nature, some people live on the strength of belief, how will you stop such people from becoming your disciples and from influencing you in establishing a faith-absorbing, useless religion? There are so many religions which advocate a process saying, "Do this and get salvation." Or, "Join us and you will be happy." Is that the type of religion you want to propagate?

Certain disciples link up with a spiritual master to fulfill a social need. Once the need is fulfilled, they go away and live their individual lives. I knew this popular spiritual master. Many young men became his disciples, but as soon as they found a wife, they went away. Some young women would come to him too. As soon as they got married, that was the end of the commitment.

People use a religious leader to acquire for themselves certain social advantages which form around him because of his stricter moral standards. How will you protect yourself from that?

There are some who become a disciple because they are in need of a father-figure. In the United States, when many youths left their parents and went here and there to various cities, and indulged in drugs and a sexually-permissive way of life, many of them became disciples of spiritual masters from India, all because they needed a parental figure. But some of the spiritual masters who accepted these Western youths, were flattered by the incidence of sudden popularity. Feeling that they were empowered, these gurus quickly mounted high seats for receiving honor. Is this your idea of becoming a spiritual master?

One spiritual master I knew, lived in an isolated place. He used to attract criminal elements and youths who rebelled against their parents and society. They went to him to escape from the pressure of the materialistic society and its strict work ethics. Gradually he took in one too many. He got involved in a criminal activity with two of them and was ruined. How will you avoid guru pitfall?

Some disciples bewitch a guru by centralizing his authority on themselves. How will you resist such disciples? For instance, I knew this important follower of a spiritual master. He was a young man with great promise for taking the monk status. Like his guru, he wanted money for pushing on their mission. Gradually he became attracted to wealthy people. He used to visit the home of a wealthy lady. I heard they got married. He became like a monkey in the cage of that lady, for she practically locked him up in her house and kept him to herself. He was no longer able to push on the mission as he used to.

First he took money from her when he was a young monk and then he was infatuated. It became romantic. He married the lady and became fixated on her. Instead of bringing her to the feet of his Lord, he went to her thighs instead. Now he lives like a rich man's parrot, locked in a big house with conveniences and meals provided.

We should not think that it is just certain spiritual masters who fall down or that we cannot fall if we assume guruship. It is neither the fallen spiritual masters nor ourselves that is the controlling factor. The controlling ingredient is the laws of material nature which may be blurred to our vision. Regardless of whom we are, these laws will take effect. Each and every one of us can become fallen if we take the post of spiritual master. Even if we do not become fallen in this life, we may, if we continue in the guru business, see ruination in the next. A big success as a guru in one life is a sure sign of a big fall in another. This is what I am saying. As limited beings, we are not suited to such a role.

Concluding Remarks

In this book, I tried to discourage guruship. I suggested that you strive for perfection and be a spiritual master without disciples. If you strive for perfection, you are a spiritual master automatically, regardless of how others define the terms. Anyone who strives for perfection is given natural authority as a leader. One does not need an institution. And most of all one does not need formal authority. Wholesome, non-destructive spiritual authority, if there is any at all, comes naturally from your endeavors, from your successes and failures while gradually extricating yourself and separating yourself from material existence, but only after you learned the lessons thoroughly and can never be drawn back into complications again.

This book is not an attempt to deride any lineage of teachers, nor any established religious institutions, but some readers may take it in that way. In fact, this book asserts the lineages and institutions by showing the real cause of their powers.

For those of you who are official spiritual masters or religious leaders, my attempt is to discourage you from expanding your influence any further and to inspire you to push on with personal development while helping others in proportion to your progression.

Lastly, I must deal with the bad tendencies of disciples. All spiritual leaders, the self-declared ones, the publicly-recognized ones, and the hidden ones, are subjected to the negative energies of disciples. In fact, if I speak to a man and just give him advice, I automatically absorb his energies; I do not have to initiate him officially as some say.

It works by a process of immediate transfer through social contact, regardless of whether that contact occurs on the material or psychic planes. I do not have to be in a disciplic succession. I do not have to be an officially recognized guru to absorb the influence of another. The only requirement is my contact with the person with intentions for giving assistance.

Success in handling bad tendencies safely, has to do with my ability to enforce disciplines in the life of the undisciplined person. If I am not powerful enough to cause that person to assume disciplines through which his vice will be curtailed, then I will be affected by it.

Bad tendencies acquired from incidental or reliable disciples are not nullified by God, as some gurus think. Or let me state it differently: These unwanted features are nullified by God only if God is the guru of the said person as Lord Krishna was the guru of Arjuna or as Jesus Christ was the guru of Peter. The vices must be nullified by the person who advises, not by his authority or by anyone else,

Thus unless you can make a person assume certain disciplines, you would be fool number one to interfere with that person. It takes an equal amount of discipline to foil an equal amount of corresponding vice. In addition, the discipline must be tailored to the particular vice.

Finally, be cautious! Stop being a con guru, a cheater, a pretense ascetic. If you cannot take a person out of the material existence, say so. Do not suggest or indicate that you can. You can still help others even if you cannot, but you should not fool the public. The least you can do is to admit that you can only take a person so far and the rest is up to God or up to higher teachers who may become available at a certain stage. In the meantime your best bet, your greatest contribution to our human condition, is this: **Your persistent and continuous purification**.

Index

M

Madhva, 21
Mahabharata, 11, 16,
              76, 105, 187,
Mahabhish, 28
Mahesh Yogi, 145
Malaysia, 49
malpractice, 223
manifest destiny, 109
manipulation, 143
Mao Tse Tung, 143, 213
Markan, 76
marriage, disciple, 202
masturbation, 206
material nature,
  control, 164
  disciple controlled by, 115
  envied, 75
  soul love affair, 70
matrimony, 202
meat, 41
menstrual cycle, 204
mental concentration, 155
mercantile people, 144
mercy energy 134
microbes, 43
milking celebrities, 146
millionaire, 125
miracles, 101
mission expansion, 57
missionary placards, 106
missionary plans, 154
Mohammed, 128, 220
monarchs, 135
money, 146, 150
monk, 67, 130
monkey, 227
Moses, 8, 88

motivation,
  bad type, 103
  change, 40
  guru affected, 150
movie star, 145
musician, 145
mystic power,
  Absolute Person's, 35
  abuse, 138
  guru's, 78, 100
  usage, 79

N

name of God, 122, 137
Nanak, 20
Nanda, 10
Napoleon, 213
Narad, 24-26, 36, 131
narcotics, 48, 146
nature attack, 104
Near East, 11
Nepal, 150
neurotic spirits, 138
New Age religions, 147
New Testament, 11, 16
New York City, 19
New York Times, 170
New Zealand, 49
Nihilistic Buddhism, 112
Nimi, 136
non-profit society, 96
nonviolence, 43
Norman Vincent Peale, 83
nudity, 28
nullify vices, 230

O

obligations, 94, 152
officialness, 224
opium, 48

Glossary of Sanskrit Names and Terms

Adi Grantha

Book which is regarded as a deity in the Sikh religion.

Advaita Vedanta

A system of philosophy in which the Absolute Truth is regarded as being non-dual, as one Reality only. Dvaita means two aspects. Advaita means one singular entity.

Ajamil

Ajamila, a deviant devotee of Krishna (Vishnu) who was pardoned from hell hereafter by the agents of Vishnu.

Akupar

Akupara, a tortoise who recognized King Indradyumna and caused that king to resume his residency in a heaven.

Arjuna

A warrior in the Kurukshetra war which is described in the Mahabharata. Arjuna became famous as the student of Krishna who was instructed in the Bhagavad Gita.

Ashvatthama

The son of Drona, the military instructor of the Kuru dynasty. See the Mahabharata.

Balarama

The elder brother of Krishna. See the Srimad Bhagavatam.

Bhagavad Gita

A discussion in the Mahabharata, which became famous as a separate literature. It is a philosophical and revelatory incidence between the lecturer who was Krishna and the inquirer who was Arjuna.

Bhagavan

A Sanskrit word meaning the Person who is God.

Bhajan

> A Sanskrit word meaning religious devotional song.
> The name of a kundalini yoga teacher.

Bhargava

> A great mystic yogi who could track departed souls and perceive
> their condition in the hereafter. He discovered the hellish
> conditions of a departed king named Shatanika.

bhastrika

> A breath system process which entails breathing rapidly with
> stress on the inhalation and exhalation. It is used to raise
> kundalini.

Bhishma

> The heroic grandsire of the Kuru dynasty. He vouched that
> Krishna was the God Vishnu. He stated that Krishna and Arjuna
> came previously as the deities Nara-Narayana. He was rated as
> being eternally liberated. He took the course of the sun during its
> ascendency to the Northern Hemisphere in order to use it to
> reach higher dimensions.
> Once during the battle of Kurukshetra, Krishna took up a chariot
> wheel to kill Bhishma's body but Arjuna stopped Krishna by
> pledging that he would kill Bhishma, who was in fact his great-
> uncle, but who has supported corrupt members of the Kuru
> family.

Bodhidharma

> This person was a Buddhist monk who crossed from China to
> India. The writer was told by his first yoga guru, Arthur
> Beverford, that Bodhidharma had introduced martial arts to
> China. Arthur Beverford was an instructor of the Ken Zen Ichii
> martial arts system.

Brahma

> A god in the Hindu pantheon. He is said to be the creator of this
> local universe.

Brahmaloka

> The residence of the god Brahma.

Buddha

> Gautama Buddha of the Shakya clan. He could not acquire
> liberation by the methods of austerity he was taught in India. He
> practiced on his own and gain full enlightenment.

Chaitanya

*He was born in Bengal, India and became known as Sri
Chaitanya Mahaprabhu. He is rated as being Krishna Himself
appearing with the complexion of Radha, one of Krishna's
milkmaid girlfriends.*

Chaitra

A month on the Hindu calendar.

Daksh

*Daksha. He is regarded as a primal progenitor but he has a
disagreement with a celestial being named Narada.*

Danta

*Dantavakra. A chieftain who lived in the time of Krishna. He was
inimical to Krishna and did not accept Krishna's claim in
aristocratic or divine status.*

Dasharatha

*He was the father of Rama. After being threatened by
Vishvamitra, he allowed Rama to go with Vishvamitra to police
religious ceremonies in the forest areas.*

Devi

*Durga Devi. She is regarded as the Woman Godhead.
She is the wife of Shiva.*

Dhruva

*A boy prince who took up gruesome yoga austerities. He was
advised by Narada on how to do yoga to reach the Vishnu Deity
on the spiritual plane. Dhruva succeeded but when he saw
Vishnu he went through a change in motive and no longer
wanted what he initially prayed for.*

Drona

*He was known as Drona, the proficient teacher. He was a
mahayogi and a person of military expertise. He instructed the
Kuru dynasty.*

Drupad

*A king who was humbled by Drona. They were friends in school
and Drupada promised to give half of his ancestral lands to
Drona but later denied the promise. Drona used the Kuru princes
to subdue Drupada. Drona then took half of Drupada's ancestral*

territory. The result was Drona's death by Drupada's son during the Battle of Kurukshetra.

Durga

She is also known as Devi, Parvati, and Jagadamba. She is regarded as the God Lady.

Duryodhana

The villain of the Mahabharata. He was a cousin of Arjuna. Even though he was shown the Universal Form of Krishna in an apparition which scared most persons who saw it, he dismissed Krishna as a mere magician.

Dvaraka

Krishna's primary city residence.

Ekalavya

An aborigine who learned the science of archery on his own, but he claimed to have learnt it from Drona by worshiping an idol form of Drona. He was discovered by Arjuna when he exhibited his skill by piecing the mouth of a dog with arrows. Subsequently he was confronted by Drona and asked to give his thumb as a guru fee.

Ganga

A demigoddess, she caused a king named Mahabhisha to lose his ascension to the higher dimension which is Brahmaloka. While entering that place, this king saw her in sheer clothing, near-nude and he could not help the sexual attraction. Subsequently he took birth on earth and reach her here as a lover.

guru

Spiritual Master. In India, a guru is expected to be in an established lineage of teachers but exceptional persons like Gautama Buddha have broken away from traditional lineages and established new lines of authority.

Guru Nanak

He established Sikhism which is really a blend of Hinduism and Islam.

Hare Krishna

This was a mantra, sound formula, given in the Kali-Santaarana Upanishad. As given there it occurs after the Hare Rama lines.

*However Sri Chaitanya gave it with the Hare Rama lines
following the Hare Krishna lines.*

*In the Kali-Santaarana recommendation, Rama may refer to
Rama of the Ramayana, but it was brought to the writer's
attention when he took initiations in a Vaishnava succession,
that Sri Chaitanya meant Balarama as Rama in the mantra.*

Hari

*Name of God in Sanskrit. This name was given to Yajna, an
incarnation of God, who rescued Manu from cannibals. It means
a person who removes all causes of distress.*

Haryas

*Haryashvas, these were sons of Daksha who were discouraged
from cultural life by Narada.*

Himalayas

*The highest mountain range in the world, located in Northern
India. It is pronounced as Him-ah-lay uh, instead of
Him-uh-lay-uh*

Hindi

*The most frequently used language in India. It is Sanskrit derived
but it has many sounds and words from other languages,
especially Arabic.*

Hinduism

*The systems of religion which are native to India. These are
collectively called Hinduism. Some religious authorities from
India do distinguish themselves as being non-Hindu.*

*Overall Hinduism is polytheistic, but though recognizing many
deities, each system usually focuses on one primal deity as the
Supreme Being.*

Indrad

*Indradyumna, the son Drupad. He was born from a fire sacrifice
and his mission was to put an end to the life of Drona. For this
he succeeded.*

Jagat guru

*Jagat means the world. Jagat guru means someone who is the
spiritual master of the world. It is a title which is usually
bestowed by disciples on their spiritual master, irrespective of
whether the spiritual master has that status in reality or not.*

Kach

> Kacha was a disciple of Brihaspati, but he was asked to get some mystic medical knowledge from the rival of Brihaspati who was Shukra. By humbly approaching Shukra, he was accepted by the teacher but he was not given the information until Shukra's life was imperiled and the teacher needed someone to revive him. Shukra's daughter Devayani had a sexual-weakness on Kacha, but when she propositioned him, he refused, saying that they were like siblings since he accepted her father as his guru. She was not pleased with that rejection.

Kashipu

> Hiranyakashipu, a dictatorial king who rejected traditional religious practices and who established himself as the supreme ruler of the earth. Initially he performed such strict austerities that he was granted an interview with Brahma, the local planetary creator. He wanted an invincible youthful body, which he attained by the grace of Brahma who sprinkled a celestial fluid on Hiranyakashipu's skeleton.

Kundalini yoga

> Yogic practice in which students are taught to activate the kundalini (life force) energy by doing various postures and breath manipulation techniques.

Kurukshetra

> A place in India, reputed as the location upon which the Battle of Kurukshetra took place, where Krishna spoke Bhagavad Gita to Arjuna.

Madhva

> Madhvacharya, a great teacher in the Vaishnava lineage. He was accepted as an authority by Chaitanya Mahaprabhu but Chaitanya rejected some of the sect's ideas.

Mahabharata

> As a word, this means the Great Legends of India (Bharata). This book is the biography of the Kauravas, the Kuru dynasty, but it has many other literatures within it. It proclaims that if something cannot be found in it, such a thing does not exist anywhere.

Mahabhisha

This king was elevated to Brahmaloka, the place of the local planetary creator according to the Vedic text. However, when he arrived there he happened to see the exposed body of the goddess Ganga when her clothes blew up by a celestial breeze. Subsequently he had to return to physical existence to reach the goddess here physically for sexual relations.

On earth he was known as King Shantanu, one of the ancestors of Arjuna.

Mahesh Yogi

He became popular in the 1960's in the western countries, because he was accepted as a meditation teacher by the Beatles. His system is called Transcendental Meditation (TM).

Markan

Markandeya. The writer first heard of this great yogin from Arthur Beverford who gave the writer a small book which was a translated excerpt from the Mahabharata. This book was published by Rishi Singh Gherwal, the guru of Arthur Beverford. It was a translation of the part of the Mahabharata, when Markandeya explained that he experienced Krishna as the Lord of universe by entering into Krishna's cosmic body many years ago. At the time Krishna floated on a Causal Ocean on a banyan leaf and his form was that of a divine baby.

Nanak

See Guru Nanak above in this table.

Nanda

A cowherd chieftain, the foster father of Krishna. He is known as Nanda Gopa.

Narad

Narada, a famous celestial authority whose name is mentioned in practically every Purana, ancient traditional religious literature. He is the son of the local creator deity Brahma.

Nihilistic Buddhism

This refers to those Buddhist Sects which do not accept deities. Buddha himself did not formally worship deities but he did acknowledge them and spoke of his meeting with them such as his meeting with many of the Brahmas, creator gods.

Nimi

A story of him is told in the Srimad Bhagavatam and in other Puranas. He was the one who asked Vasishtha Rishi to perform a sacrifice and who was told to postpone the ceremony for a later date. He was very anxious to do the sacrifice on a specific auspicious date but Vasishtha did not think it was a priority. Nimi then engaged another priest and when this was discovered by Vasishtha he cursed Nimi, who cursed the guru priest in turn.

Pandavas

These were the sons of King Pandu. Arjuna was the third of the five sons.

pranam

It is said as a customary greeting in the Hindu community. It means that one person is offering his or her religious or devotional respects to another person.

pranayama

The fourth stage of yoga, which has eight stages. It has to do with breath manipulation.

Prithu

A king who performed austerities in his youth and who completed his life to spiritual perfection in the elderly years. He took advice from Narada and the Kumaras. He saw the celestial form of Brahma directly.

Priyavarta

A king who was a Mahayogin and who is said to have exhibited cosmic creative powers.

Prtha

Prtha, the mother of Arjuna. Her other name is Kunti.

Punjabi

A person who took birth in Punjab, India.

Purana

There are 18 principal Puranas but there is a contention that the best of the Puranas is the Srimad Bhagavatam. However in some parts of India, the Devi Purana is considered to be the best and in other parts, the Bhagavata Purana is regarded as foremost. There are also subsidiary texts which are known as Upa Puranas. One important feature of the Puranas, at least the 18 principal ones, is that they are said to have been written by the same person who is called Vyasa. Vyasa however is a title and not the name of a particular person. But the person who was the son of Parashar Muni, and who was known as Dvaipayana, is said to be the Vyasa who wrote the principal Puranas.

Each Purana presents a particular deity as the Supreme Person, such that in the Shiva Purana, Shiva is presented as the Supreme Being and in the Bhagavata Purana of the Vaishnavas, Krishna is presented as such, while in the Devi Purana, Devi Durga is presented as the Absolute Lady God.

Rajnesh

This person set up a spiritual society in Washington state in the United States but he came to ruin when Federal authorities investigated his sect and forced him to leave the United States. He was a Jain at one stage of his life. After some transcendental experiences he separated himself from that and began functioning as an independent guru.

Rama

This person is rated as a Personality of Godhead, His biography is given to us in the Sri Ramayana of Valmiki. In the author's opinion his actions in that book are conclusive proof of his divinity. He is known by many through a book known as the Ramcharita Manas which was written by Tulsie das Gosvami, but that book deviated from the Valmiki Ramayana which is the original reference.

Ramayana

There are several Ramayanas. The original one is by Valmiki, and is recommended by the author of this book.

Ravan

Ravana, he is the villain of the Ramayana. Rama defeated and killed him after he abducted Rama's wife, Sita.

Revat

Revata was a king in the time of Krishna. His significance there is that his daughter was married to Krishna's elder brother, Balarama.

Revata, in a previous life as a king, is said to have been transferred out of this dimension and went to Brahma's world. He took his daughter on the journey because he wanted to marry her to an exalted person. On Brahma's planet he found out that *there was a time warp of thousands of years in reference to the earth, but as it turned out he was able to offer his daughter to Lord Balarama when he returned to the earth.*

Sahasranik

Sahasranika was the son of King Shatanika. This son challenged the priest who officiated for the government. He wanted them to show definitely where his father had travelled to in the hereafter. Under pressure from him, the priests engaged Rishi Bhargava to find the departed king who was transferred to a hell.

Sanat

Sanat Kumara is one of the four special sons of Brahma who retain boyhood forms but with adult mental capacity. They are rated as empowered souls. They are masters of mystic yoga and were able to see into the transcendental dimensions.

sannyasi

This is a celibate monk. Previously a sannyasi did not get involved in having disciples and missions but now sannyasis do just that.

A sannyasi takes a vow for lifelong celibacy and it used to be that if he broke his vow he was expected to kill his body in Ganges.

Sanskrit

A language of India. Most of the traditional Indian Scriptures and yoga texts are written in Sanskrit. This language is sometimes called devanagari which means the language of the gods. The work sanskrita means something tht is well organized or well done.

Satyananda

This was a yogi guru. He was a disciple of Swami Shivananda.

Savalas

Sons of Daksha who were diverted from family life by Narada. This is described in the Srimad Bhagavatam.

Shaktipat

A power infusement into a disciple, done so by a guru. It has varying effects depending on the nature of the disciple and the intention of the guru.

Shatanik

Shatanika, the king who went to a hellish place in the hereafter because he used government funds to finance religious ceremonies. He was discovered by Bhargava Yogin.

Shishu

Shishupala, he was inimical to Krishna. He wanted to marry Rukmini, who was kidnapped by Krishna upon request. He denounced Krishna during an award ceremony, when Krishna was given the prime honor as the Best of the Personalities. Because he behaved boisterously and was enraged, he was killed by Krishna during the ceremony.

Shiva

Shiva is considered to be one of the three primal deities in the Hindu Pantheon of Deities. The other two are Brahma and Vishnu.

In the Shiva Purana, Shiva is presented as the Supreme Being over all other deities in the Vedic Pantheon.

His wife is Devi, Durga, the Woman God.

Shiva Purana

The main scriptures which advocate Shiva as Supreme God.

Shivananda

A celibate yogi monk, who established the divine life society. He is a Mahayogin.

Shukra

Shukracharya was a capable mystic yogin but he was indifferent to the godly celestial and took side with their opponents. His expertise was mystic medical procedure, which he was circumstantially pressured to reveal to Kacha who was a spy of his opponents.

Sikhism

This is a religious system in India, which is prevalent in Punjab. It was founded by Guru Nanak and in the author's opinion it is a combination of Hinduism and Islam but it leaves aside the idol worship which is a prominent feature of Hinduism.

siddhi

This is a power or skill of the subtle body.

Subahu

A brother of Maricha, who took the form of a golden deer which was used as a lure by Ravana to distract Rama and Laksmana. Subahu, along with his mother Tatika, was killed by Rama by the requiest of Vishvamitra. Maricha was wounded at the same time but he survived and was later killed by Rama when he took the form of a golden deer and caused Rama and Laksman to be diverted while Ravana kidnapped Princess Sita.

Upanishad

The Upanishads are a set of writings by some ancient yogi sages, whose ideas which are echoed in the Bhagavad Gita.

Vaishnava

A person who accepts Vishnu as the Supreme Being.

Vasisht

Vasishtha is a famous rishi. He was challenged by King Vishvamitra and defeated that king when the rishi's cow produced soldiers and weapons to vanquish the king's army. Seeing this, the king vowed to renounce his royal status and become an ascetic yogi.

Vasudeva

The biological father of Krishna, who was raised by his foster father, Nanda Gopa. .

Veda

Veda is said to be the first and original scripture. It is known to be of four parts, namely the Rig, Sama, Yajur and Atharva.

Vedanta

This literally means the end (anta) of knowledge (Veda). The whole range of philosophical information from Indian sages is called Vedanta collectively but each sect defines the term differently.

Vishnu

One of the three principal deities in the Hindu Pantheon of deities. The other two primal ones are Brahma and Shiva. Those who accept Vishnu as the Supreme Being are known as Vaishnavas. Those who accept Shiva are known as Shivaites.Those who accept Devi Durga are known as Shaktas Brahma is not taken as seriously as Shiva and Vishnu.

Vishnudevananda

A hatha yoga guru of the writer. Swami Vishnudevananda wrote many authoritative books on Ashtanga Yoga and did much teaching before he departed from his body. He was a prominent disciple of Swami Shivananda. One of his main contributions was a translation and commentary of the Hatha Yoga Pradipika.

Vishwa

Vishwamitra was the king who attained brahmin rishi status by his sheer endeavor. It took him some time but he achieved it without having to change bodies. Usually one cannot do this, except over a period of many lives.

Vivekananda

This was one of the first Swamis to become popular in the West. He was a disciple of Ramakrishna Paramhansa. He wrote many books.

Vyasa

The reputed author of the Puranas is Krishna Dvaipayana Vyasa who was actually the grandfather of Arjuna.

He is accredited as having divided the One Veda into four parts.

yoga

This word has come to mean many things but Patanjali defines yoga as an eight part system consisting of yama, niyama, asana, pranayama, pratyahar, dharana, dhyana and samadhi.

Many people define yoga in terms of its Sanskrit root word which is yuj and which means to unify or to yoke.

Yogananda

Paramhansa Yogananda was a famous yogi who established the Self Realization Fellowship in the United States. He publicized the kriya yoga system which was taught by Sri Babaji Mahayogin. His book, Autobiography of a Yogi, was an inspiration to millions of human beings to begin them on the quest of finding spiritual identity.

Yogesh

Yogeshwarananda Vyasji Mahayogin. This person is a dear spiritual master of the writer. Yogeshwarananda wrote many books, one of which is Science of the Soul.

The author cannot in any way repay him for the techniques he reveals on the astral plane.

Yogi Bhajan

This is a kundalini yoga master, from whom the writer learned the bhastrika pranayama method of kundalini yoga. This is a rapid method for causing kundalini to be cooperative with one's spiritual aspirations.

Yogiji established the 3HO Foundation during the life of his recent body. He is now departed but the writer keeps in contact with him on the astral planes.

Author

Michael Beloved (Madhvacharya das) took his current body in 1951 in Guyana. In 1965, while living in Trinidad, he instinctively began doing yoga postures and trying to make sense of the supernatural side of life.

Later on, in 1970, in the Philippines, he approached a Martial Arts Master named Mr. Arthur Beverford, explaining to the teacher that he was seeking a yoga instructor. Mr. Beverford identified himself as an advanced disciple of Sri Rishi Singh Gherwal, an ashtanga yoga master.

Mr. Beverford taught the traditional ashtanga yoga with stress on postures, attentive breathing and brow chakra centering meditation. In 1972, Michael entered the Denver Colorado Ashram of Kundalini Yoga Master Sri Harbhajan Singh. There he took instruction in Bhastrika Pranayama and its application to yoga postures. He was supervised mostly by Yogi Bhajan's disciple named Prem Kaur.

In 1979 Michael formally entered the disciplic succession of the Brahma-Madhva Gaudiya Sampradaya through Swami Kirtanananda, who was a prominent sannyasi disciple of the Great Vaishnava Authority Sri Swami Bhaktivedanta Prabhupada, the exponent of devotion to Sri Krishna.

Apart from this, Michael took instructions from proficient gurus on the astral planes. For producing this publication, Michael reviewed his diaries to gain information about spiritual masters and disciples.

Publications

English Series

Bhagavad Gita English

Anu Gita English

Markandeya Samasya English

Yoga Sutras English

Uddhava Gita English

These are in 21st Century English, very precise and exacting. Many Sanskrit words which were considered untranslatable into a Western language are rendered in precise, expressive and modern English, due to the English language becoming the world's universal means of concept conveyance.

Three of these books are instructions from Krishna. **In Bhagavad Gita English** and **Anu Gita English**, the instructions were for Arjuna. In the **Uddhava Gita English,** it was for Uddhava. Bhagavad Gita and Anu Gita are extracted from the Mahabharata. Uddhava Gita was extracted from the 11th Canto of the Srimad Bhagavatam

(Bhagavata Purana). One of these books, the **Markandeya Samasya English** is about Krishna, as described by Yogi Markandeya, who survived the cosmic collapse and reached a divine child in whose transcendental body, the collapsed world was existing. Another of these books, the **Yoga Sutras English,** is the detailed syllabus about yoga practice.

My suggestion is that you read **Bhagavad Gita English**, the **Anu Gita English, the Markandeya Samasya English,** the **Yoga Sutras English** and lastly the **Uddhava Gita English**, which is much more complicated and detailed.

For each of these books we have at least one commentary, which is published separately. Thus your particular interest can be researched further in the commentaries.

The smallest of these commentaries and perhaps the simplest is the one for the Anu Gita. We published its commentary as the Anu Gita Explained. The Bhagavad Gita explanations were published in three distinct targeted commentaries. The first is Bhagavad Gita Explained, which sheds lights on how people in the time of Krishna and Arjuna regarded the information and applied it. Bhagavad Gita is an exposition of the application of yoga practice to cultural activities, which is known in the Sanskrit language as karma yoga.

Interestingly, Bhagavad Gita was spoken on a battlefield just before one of the greatest battles in the ancient world. A warrior, Arjuna, lost his wits and had no idea that he could apply his training in yoga to political dealings. Krishna, his charioteer, lectured on the spur of the moment to give Arjuna the skill of using yoga proficiency in cultural dealings including how to deal with corrupt officials on a battlefield.

The second commentary is the Kriya Yoga Bhagavad Gita. This clears the air about Krishna's information on the science of kriya yoga, showing that its techniques are clearly described free of charge to anyone who takes the time to read Bhagavad Gita.

Kriya yoga concerns the battlefield which is the psyche of the living being. The internal war and the mental and emotional forces which are hostile to self-realization are dealt with in the kriya yoga practice.

The third commentary is the Brahma Yoga Bhagavad Gita. This shows what Krishna had to say outright and what he hinted about which concerns the brahma yoga practice, a mystic process for those who mastered kriya yoga.

There is one commentary for the **Markandeya Samasya English**. The title of that publication is Krishna Cosmic Body.

There are two commentaries to the Yoga Sutras. One is the Yoga Sutras of Patanjali and the other is the Meditation Expertise. These give detailed explanations of the process of Yoga.

For the Uddhava Gita, we published the Uddhava Gita Explained. This is a large book and requires concentration and study for integration of the information. Of the books which deal with transcendental topics, my opinion is that the discourse between Krishna and Uddhava has the complete information about the realities in existence. This book is the one which removes massive existential ignorance.

Meditation Series

Meditation Pictorial

Meditation Expertise

Core-Self Discovery

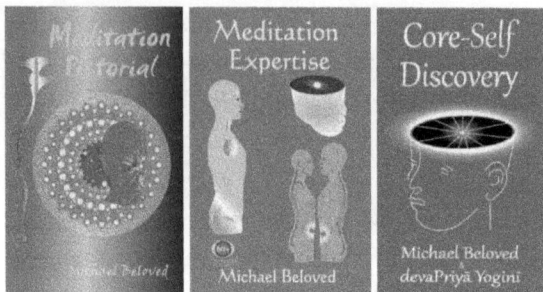

The specialty of these books is the mind diagrams which profusely illustrate what is written. This shows exactly what one has to do mentally to develop and then sustain a meditation practice.

In the **Meditation Pictorial**, one is shown how to develop psychic insight, a feature without which meditation is imagination and visualization, without any mystic experience per se.

In the **Meditation Experti**se, one is shown how to corral one's practice to bring it in line with the classic syllabus of yoga which Patanjali lays out as the ashtanga yoga eight-staged practice.

In **Core-Self Discovery**, one is taken though the course of pratyahar sensual energy withdrawal which is the 5th stage of yoga in the Patanjali ashtanga eight-process complete system of yoga practice. These events lead to the discovery of a core-self which is surrounded by psychic organs in the head of the subtle body. This product has a DVD component for teachers and self-teaching students.

These books are profusely illustrated with mind diagrams showing the components of psychic consciousness and the inner design of the subtle body.

Explained Series

Bhagavad Gita Explained

Uddhava Gita Explained

Anu Gita Explained

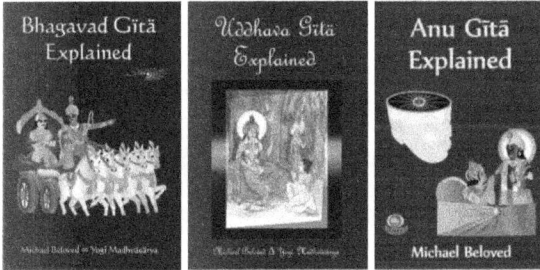

The specialty of these books is that they are free of missionary intentions, cult tactics and philosophical distortion. Instead of using these books to add credence to a philosophy, meditation process, belief or plea for followers, I spread the information out so that a reader can look through this literature and freely take or leave anything as desired.

When Krishna stressed himself as God, I stated that. When Krishna laid no claims for supremacy, I showed that. The reader is left to form an independent opinion about the validity of the information and the credibility of Krishna.

There is a difference in the discourse with Arjuna in the Bhagavad Gita and the one with Uddhava in the Uddhava Gita. In fact these two books may appear to contradict each other. In the Bhagavad Gita, Krishna pressured Arjuna to complete social duties. In the Uddhava Gita, Krishna insisted that Uddhava should abandon the same.

The Anu Gita is not as popular as the Bhagavad Gita but it is the conclusion of that text. Anu means what is to follow, what proceeds. In this discourse, an anxious Arjuna request that Krishna should repeat the Bhagavad Gita and again show His supernatural and divine forms.

However Krishna refuses to do so and chastises Arjuna for being a disappointment in forgetting what was revealed. Krishna then cites a celestial yogi, a near-perfected being, who explained the process of transmigration in vivid detail.

Commentaries

Yoga Sutras of Patanjali

Meditation Expertise

Krishna Cosmic Body

Anu Gita Explained

Bhagavad Gita Explained

Kriya Yoga Bhagavad Gita

Brahma Yoga Bhagavad Gita

Uddhava Gita Explained

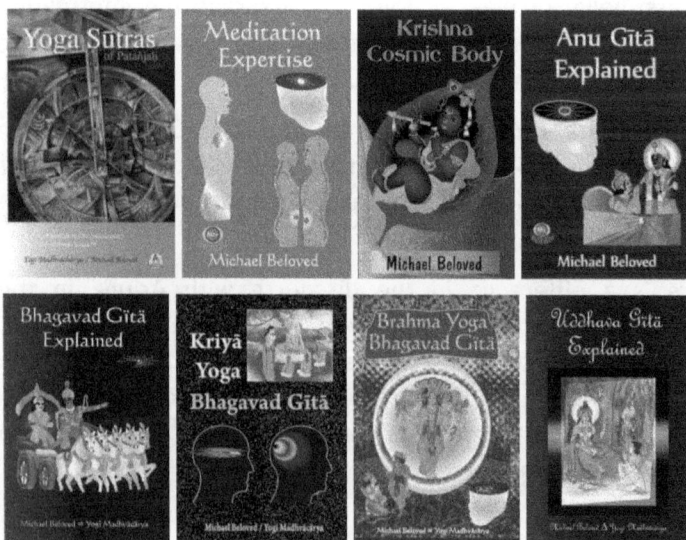

Yoga Sutras of Patanjali is the globally acclaimed text book of yoga. This has detailed expositions of yoga techniques. Many kriya techniques are vividly described in the commentary.

Meditation Expertise is an analysis and application of the Yoga Sutras. This book is loaded with illustrations and has detailed explanations of secretive advanced meditation techniques which are called kriyas in the Sanskrit language.

Krishna Cosmic Body is a narrative commentary on the Markandeya Samasya portion of the Aranyaka Parva of the Mahabharata. This is the detailed description of the dissolution of the world, as experienced by the great yogin Markandeya who transcended the cosmic deity, Brahma, and reached Brahma's source who is the divine infant, Krishna.

Anu Gita Explained is a detailed explanation of how we endure many material bodies in the course of transmigrating through various life-forms. This is a discourse between Krishna and Arjuna. Arjuna requested of Krishna a display of the Universal Form and a repeat narration of the Bhagavad Gita but Krishna declined and explained what a siddha perfected being told the Yadu family about the sequence of existences one endures and the systematic flow of those lives at the convenience of material nature.

Bhagavad Gita Explained shows what was said in the Gita without religious overtones and sectarian biases.

Kriya Yoga Bhagavad Gita shows the instructions for those who are doing kriya yoga.

Brahma Yoga Bhagavad Gita shows the instructions for those who are doing brahma yoga.

Uddhava Gita Explained shows the instructions to Uddhava which are more advanced than the ones given to Arjuna.

Bhagavad Gita is an instruction for applying the expertise of yoga in the cultural field. This is why the process taught to Arjuna is called karma yoga which means karma + yoga or cultural activities done with a yogic demeanor.

Uddhava Gita is an instruction for apply the expertise of yoga to attaining spiritual status. This is why it is explains jnana yoga and bhakti yoga in detail. Jnana yoga is using mystic skill for knowing the spiritual part of existence. Bhakti yoga is for developing affectionate relationships with divine beings.

Karma yoga is for negotiating the social concerns in the material world and therefore it is inferior to bhakti yoga which concerns negotiating the social concerns in the spiritual world.

This world has a social environment and the spiritual world has one too.

Right now Uddhava Gita is the most advanced informative spiritual book on the planet. There is nothing anywhere which is superior to it or which goes into so much detail as it. It verified that historically Krishna is the most advanced human being to ever have left literary instructions on this planet. Even Patanjali Yoga Sutras which I translated and gave an application for in my book, **Meditation Expertise**, does not go as far as the Uddhava Gita.

Some of the information of these two books is identical but while the Yoga Sutras are concerned with the personal spiritual emancipation (kaivalyam) of the individual spirits, the Uddhava Gita explains that and also explains the situations in the spiritual universes.

Bhagavad Gita is from the Mahabharata which is the history of the Pandavas. Arjuna, the student of the Gita, is one of the Pandavas brothers. He was in a social hassle and did not know how to apply yoga expertise to solve it. Krishna gave him a crash-course on the battlefield about that.

Uddhava Gita is from the Srimad Bhagavatam (Bhagavata Purana), which is a history of the incarnations of Krishna. Uddhava was a relative of Krishna. He was concerned about the situation of the deaths of many of his relatives but Krishna diverted Uddhava's attention to the practice of yoga for the purpose of successfully migrating to the spiritual environment.

Specialty

These books are based on the author's experiences in meditation, yoga practice and participation in spiritual groups:

Spiritual Master

sex you!

Sleep **Paralysis**

Astral Projection

Masturbation Psychic Details

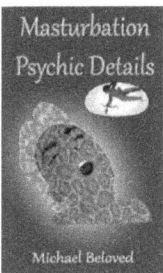

In **Spiritual Master**, Michael draws from experience with gurus or with their senior students. His contact with astral gurus is rated. He walks you through the avenue of gurus showing what you should do and what you should not do, so as to gain proficiency in whatever area of spirituality the guru has proficiency.

sex you! is a masterpiece about the adventures of an individual spirit's passage through the parents' psyches. The conversion of a departed soul into a sexual urge is described. The transit from the afterlife to residency in the emotions of the parents is detailed. This is about sex and you; learn about how much of you comprises the romantic energy of your would-be parents!

Sleep Paralysis clears misconceptions so that one can see what sleep paralysis is and what frightening astral experience occurs while the paralysis is being experienced. This disempowerment has great value in giving you confidence that you can and do exist even if you are unable to operate the physical body. The implication is that one can exist apart from and will survive the loss of the material body.

Astral Projection details experiences Michael had even in childhood, where he assumed incorrectly that everyone was astrally conversant. He discusses the life force psychic mechanism which operates the sleep-wake cycle of the physical form, and which budgets energy into the separated astral form which determines if the individual will have dream recall or no objective awareness during the projections. Astral travel happens on every occasion when the physical body sleeps. What is missing in awareness is the observer status while the astral body is separated.

Masturbation Psychic Details is a surprise presentation which relates what happens on the psychic plane during a masturbation event. This does not tackle moral issues or even addictions but shows the involvement of memory and the sure but hidden subconscious mind which operates many features of the psyche irrespective of the desire or approval of the self-conscious personality.

Online Resources

Visit The Website And Forum

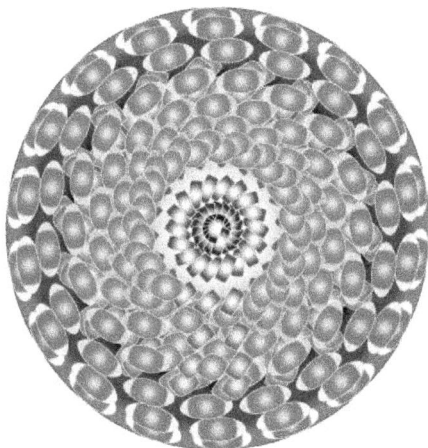

Email:	michaelbelovedbooks@gmail.com
	axisnexus@gmail.com
Website	michaelbeloved.com
Forum:	inselfyoga.com